CACTI
SUCCULENTS
& TROPICAL
PLANTS

Edited by Nicky Hayden

Distributed in the United States by Amiel Book Distributors,
31 West 46th Street, New York NY 10036

Published by Marshall Cavendish Publications Limited,
58 Old Compton Street, London W1V 5PA

This volume first published 1975

Printed in Great Britain by
Severn Valley Press Limited

ISBN 0 8148 0646 5

Introduction

Cacti and other succulents are fascinating plants to grow and they are becoming increasingly popular. Even if you don't have a greenhouse or conservatory you can build up a collection of plants in your own home and still derive a great deal of satisfaction from them. Many species don't need a lot of heat – some can be grown in the rock garden or border. And, unlike most other plants, they can thrive on a very intermittent supply of water!

Tropical plants can also give pleasure if you are prepared to give them a bit more attention – greenhouse treatment is generally necessary but the results can be literally fantastic, with beautiful and exotic blooms which will be the envy of all your friends! This book gives all the basic information you will need to care for cacti and other succulents, and many types of tropical flowers. Lists of plants, chosen for their general availability as well as their attractive appearance, are included with hints on their individual cultivation.

Contents

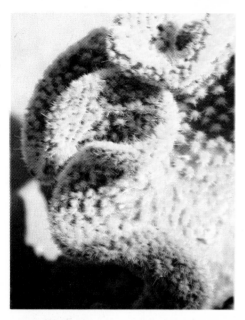

Below: Cacti are not difficult to cultivate. Even a small collection can give immense satisfaction, and it is not always necessary to have a special greenhouse to keep them in.
Far left: Opuntia microdasys cristata, the crested form that illustrates the word 'cristate'. Various different plants produce this compressed growth.
Left: Most cacti can manage with little water, but Zygocactus truncatus needs moderate water and a constant temperature of 60°F (16°C).

Growing cacti and other succulents

The growing and collecting of cacti and succulents has been a popular hobby in this country for many years. Their varied shapes and colours together with the coloured spines make them fascinating and their spectacular flowers are an added interest for the grower. Some of the larger types may not flower without very strong and prolonged sunshine, but many hundreds of other species should flower every year.

The growing of succulent plants is much easier than the cultivation of most pot plants. These plants are found in nature in districts where there is either little rainfall or the rain is limited to two or three months in the year, and so they are able to withstand considerable drought. By the composition of their skin covering they can conserve the moisture in their leaves or stems and do not wither or droop when they do not get watered.

There are many different species of succulents, many of which are erroneously called cacti. All cacti are succulents but not all succulents are cacti. Spines are found on all true cacti and these spines grown from a small tuft of hair or wool. This is know as an areole and no other plant has it. No cacti have leaves except the genus *Pereskia*. This plant has areoles and leaves and also a multiple flower, unlike true cacti which have a simple or single flower. The flowers of cacti have no stem or stalk, the ovary being connected directly with the plant. Exceptions to this rule are the Pereskias. Most cacti come from Mexico and the southern States of the USA, and also from many countries in South America, including Peru, Paraguay, Uruguay, Chile and Brazil. A few are found in the West Indies but none in Africa, India or anywhere in the east. South Africa is the home of very many of the other succulent genera grown by collectors.

Flowering cacti Some species flower the year after the seed has been sown, while very many more can produce flowers within two years. As the native habitats of these plants are arid regions it is essential that they be allowed all the sunshine possible to enable them to grow at their best.

The flowers of most cacti are formed at the areole but a few genera produce flowers away from this point. Plants of the genus *Mammillaria* produce their flowers at the axil, the spot between the tubercles. This genus also makes new plants or offsets at the axil as well,

whereas most cacti make offsets at an areole. The flowers of cacti vary considerably in size from $\frac{1}{3}$ inch in some mammillarias to 14 inches across in some of the night-flowering types. The larger flowers may not be produced in profusion but some of the cacti with smaller flowers can have rings of flowers all round the top of the plants for months at a time.

Cacti and succulents are often described as desert plants but this is not quite true. Many are found in prairie type country where there may be a few small trees and shrubs with coarse grasses intermingled. Some are found in good loam while others are found growing on rocks and the mountain side. Some of the best flowering cacti, the epiphyllums, grow in the forests of Brazil, usually on trees. Such cacti are classed as epiphytes or epiphytic cacti.

Cactus cultivation

As cacti vary so much in size from perhaps 1 inch to 30 feet or more there are many species available to the grower to suit almost any situation or condition. Although the best place to grow a collection of cacti is in a greenhouse, there are many kinds which can be grown quite well in a sunny window.

Although all cacti can go for long periods without water, it is essential that they are provided with an adequate supply during the growing period or they cannot flourish.

To grow cacti well, and flower them, it is imperative to provide them with a porous soil as the roots soon rot if they are wet for days on end. Many types of potting soils could be used and recommended, even different ones for each genus; it is possible, however, to grow practically all types of cacti in one kind of potting compost. The art of growing cacti is in the watering and the amount given can vary according to the type of compost. Plants can only obtain their nourishment in a liquid form. Only small quantities of water should be given, this will ensure that they receive correct nourishment.

Potting composts A very good potting compost for cacti may be made up from a compost with few added nutrients, to which is added a sixth part of coarse sand to make it more porous. Some additions of broken brick or granulated charcoal may be incorporated in the added sand. If it is desired to mix a compost for general use, the following will be found quite reliable. Take 2 parts

of loam, 1 part of peat and 1 part of sharp, coarse sand. Mix well and to each bushel add $\frac{3}{4}$ oz of ground chalk or limestone $\frac{3}{4}$ oz sulphate of potash, $1\frac{1}{2}$ oz of superphosphate and $1\frac{1}{2}$ oz of hoof and horn grist. All the globular and columnar types of cacti may be grown in this compost, while for the epiphytes some average branded potting compost may be used, as these plants will benefit from the richer soil. The very spiny types of cacti do not require heavy feeding with fertilisers and as long as they are repotted at least every two years they will grow quite well. If these plants are fed too liberally they will become lush, open in texture, and be very liable to rot off in the winter. Also it will be found that the spines formed when the plant has been fed with fertilisers may not be as stout and well coloured as if the plant had been grown harder. When making up the cactus compost it is very important to find a good loam as a basis for the mixture. An ideal type is the top spit from an old-standing meadow. Unfortunately these meadows are becoming few and far between and the loam is often only the under spit after the top turf has been removed. The peat is not so important but the sand must be very sharp and coarse. Silver sand is useless for cactus compost and the type known as washed grit, or river grit is the best.

The potting compost should not be used immediately after it has been mixed and a lapse of a fortnight at least is desirable before potting. The time to repot varies considerably, being determined by many factors. Some cacti are very slow growers and so may be left in their pots for two or three years while others may need a move twice a year. Many cacti never flower because they have been in the same stale, worn-out soil for many years. With fairly frequent watering during the growing period the roots of the plant use up the nourishment in the soil, and clearly there can be little food value left in it after about a year.

Repotting The best time for repotting is during the growing period, which with most cacti will be between March and September. Once new growth is seen on a plant it can be repotted. When dealing with a fairly large collection it will be found better to make a start with the larger pots. These can then be cleaned for use with other plants which may need a bigger pot. It is also a good plan to make a clear place in the greenhouse and place all repotted plants there so that none may be missed. The pots should be clean and well crocked. It is unnecessary to place a large number of crocks in the pot as they will only take up valuable space which would be better occupied by good soil. The best way to crock a pot for a cactus is to cut as large a piece of broken flower pot as will lie in the bottom of the pot. This large crock will then form a kind of platform when the plant is removed the next time. If a stick is pushed up through the drainage hole the crock will force the whole ball of soil up in the pot, whereas if a number of small pieces of crock are used it is possible to damage the roots when trying to remove the plant another time.

Place some of the coarsest particles of compost over the crock and then a little soil. Remove the plant from the old pot and hold it by the root system. Gently work all the old soil away from the roots. If any appear dead they should be cut-away. Now rest the plant in the pot and gradually work in some fresh compost. Because most of the plants are spiny it may not be possible to work the soil in with the hands as is possible with ordinary plants. A tablespoon can be used to insert the soil and it can be gently firmed in with an old table-knife handle. A wooden stick must not be used as it would catch in the spines and break them. Once a spine is broken it will never grow again. See that the plant is in the same relative position in the soil as it was before. See also that at least ½ inch of space is left at the top of the pot for watering. The plant should look right in the new pot; do not use one too large so that the plant looks lost or one so small that there is no room for soil as well as the base and roots of the plant. For the globular kinds of cacti a pot which is 12 mm (½ inch) bigger all round than the plant will do for pots up to 88 mm (3½ inches) in diameter, but for a larger plant a pot at least 25 mm (1 inch) larger all round must be provided. This will not be sufficient for many of the taller growing types as the pot must be large enough to form a firm base to stop the plant and pot from falling over.

Plastic pots may be used, especially for small plants; they do not appear to dry out as quickly as clay pots. Once the plant is potted it is important to insert the label, and a good plan is to put the date of repotting on the back. This is a useful guide in a large collection. As it is essential that the soil should be able to discharge all surplus water as soon as

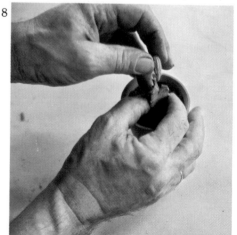

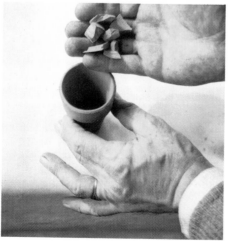

1 Preparing a pot before sowing cactus seeds. 2 Sowing the seeds. 3 The seedlings have appeared. 4 Crocking a pot for drainage before pricking out the seedlings. 5 Pricking out the tiny seedlings. 6 Potting a large specimen, using a spoon to place compost round the plant. 7 Firming the soil. 8 Grafting a cactus.

possible, the pots should not be stood on a flat surface. Some coarse gravel makes an ideal base on which to stand the pots. If slats are provided in the greenhouse it is better to cover them with corrugated asbestos sheeting on which the gravel may be placed. Any plants stood on shelves must have a saucer containing gravel under them to allow the free removal of surplus water.

Watering cacti Watering the plant presents the most important part of cactus culture. More plants are lost through overwatering than from any other cause. As has been stated before, cacti will not grow without water but if they get too much they can soon die. Newly potted cacti should not need watering for about a week. The potting soil should have been crumbly moist at the time of moving the plant. If it is too wet or too dry it cannot be firmed in the correct manner. The whole secret of watering can be described in one sentence. Never water a plant if the soil is still damp. It is not easy to tell when a cactus needs watering. Ordinary plants soon show by drooping leaves when water is required, but cacti cannot show their needs in this way. The condition of the top of the soil will indicate when water is needed. After a hot day the soil may appear dry, but this may only be the top inch. If pots are inspected in the mornings the soil should be of a uniform dampness throughout.

Rain water is better than tap water but if rain water is not available let some tap water stand in the open for a day or two before it is used. Water may be given from a can with a small spout so that it can be directed into any pot. Do not water by immersion except for the first watering after the winter. If plants are watered this way often, all the nourishing matter will soon be washed out of the pot. Cacti may be sprayed in the evening of a hot day. No water need be given from the end of September to early March. Then water when the soil has dried out, not before. The Christmas cactus, *Zygocactus truncatus*, may be watered during the winter as long as the temperature is not below 50°F (10°C). Other cacti may be left at 40°F (4°C), so that they get a winter's rest.

Taking cuttings Propagation is by cuttings, taking offsets or by seed raising. Cuttings taken from opuntias and epiphyllums are removed with a sharp knife and the cut part is allowed to dry in the sun. The cuttings are then rested on a mixture of equal parts of peat and sharp sand (not silver sand). Cactus

Top: Echinocactus, Opuntia and Mammillaria form part of a collection of cacti and other succulents.
Centre: Brilliantly colourful when in flower, cacti are not difficult to raise from seed.
Bottom: Very tolerant of neglect, cacti are becoming increasingly popular as house plants for sunny window-ledges.

potting compost may be used to fill three quarters of the pot, with the rooting medium on top. Place in a sunny position and spray occasionally. Too much water must not be given until roots have formed. Tall cuttings will have to be supported by a stick, as they must not be pushed into the medium.

Grafting Grafting may be done to assist the growth of a small, slow-growing type. A tall type is used for the stock, such as *Trichocereus spachianus*. The top is cut from the stock where the growth is new and healthy. The scion is cut at the base so that it is about the size of the top of the stock. It is brought in contact with the freshly cut stock and kept in position with two small weights on a piece of string, pressing the scion down firmly. Keep in the shade for a week or two and a firm joint will form.

Raising cacti from seed Some cacti never make offsets and these have to be raised from seed. A small propagating frame can easily be made and heated with an electric cable or even an electric lamp. Half-pots of about 4 inches in diameter are very good for sowing small quantities of seed. They can even be divided with celluloid labels if more than one species is to be sown in the pot. Use a good seed compost and sieve a small quantity through a perforated zinc sieve. Place the coarse material over the crock and then top up with ordinary compost, having an inch of the fine soil on top. Small seed must not be buried, but fairly large seeds can be just pushed into the soil. Water the first time by standing in containers of water so that the whole soil can be well moistened. Place in the frame with a piece of glass on top and then cover with dark paper. The best time to sow is in early spring, in a temperature of 70°F (21°C); seeds will germinate at a lower temperature but will take longer to do so. Once seedlings have appeared, the paper must be removed and the glass should be raised slightly. The seedlings must be kept from the direct sun for the first year but they must have plenty of light or they will become drawn. Do not allow the seed pots to dry out while germination is taking place; watering may be done with a fine spray.

Prick out when the cotyledon or food-bag has been absorbed. Before this the root is so tiny that it can be broken very easily, in which case the seedling would die. The seedlings may be placed 1 inch apart in the cactus compost as described above. Do not pot up too soon into small pots as these dry out very quickly. Boxes made of concrete or plastic are better for the seedlings until they are ready to go into 2 inch pots.

Summer treatment Cacti may be planted out in beds from June to September. If they are removed from their pots it may be quite impossible to put them back in the same sized pots in the late summer or autumn. They may be left in

Top: Mammillaria geminispina.
Above: Aporocactus flagelliformis, the Rat-tailed Cactus. Both these are easy to grow on a sunny window-sill and should produce flowers regularly each year.

their pots, but the drainage hole must be freed from soil when they are removed. A few cacti may stand the cold of winter out of doors, but a very severe winter would probably kill them. If the grower wishes to experiment, he should make sure that any cacti left out during the winter are those which can be parted with, and not specimen plants.

All the spiny types of cacti can stand plenty of sunshine as long as there is plenty of air available in a greenhouse. The epiphytes benefit from shade during the hotter months of the year, and may be stood outside the greenhouse provided no frosts are forecast. Cacti kept in windows of the house must be where they can get the maximum amount of light and they will not flower well unless they can get a fair amount of sunshine.

Most cacti flower in spring, summer or autumn, and it will be found that many flower on new growth only. If the flowers are pollinated many colourful seed pods can be formed. On the mammillarias these pods can look very attractive.

Pests If cacti are grown well they suffer little disease but there are a few pests which may attack a sick plant. The most

frequent is the mealy bug. This appears in a small tuft of wool or powder. Scale may also attack some cacti and looks like a small scab. Red spider may be a nuisance if the atmosphere is too dry. All these pests can be killed with malathion, used as directed on the bottle.

Cultivating other succulents
Most succulents thrive in the same conditions as given for cacti, so it is only necessary to give the few exceptions special treatment to be able to grow them all in one greenhouse. Those which may present some difficulty in a mixed collection are the 'mimicry' types which are found in South Africa. Many of these have a particular resting period and unless this is copied in cultivation it is probable that the plants will grow out of character. Those mimicry plants of the mesembryanthemum group, such as lithops and conophytums, are better placed by themselves in the greenhouse where they can be given specially required treatment with regard to watering, etc. Some succulents do not require as much direct sunshine as others. It may be possible to site these in the greenhouse where they are able to get partial shade, perhaps from taller-growing plants.

Some of the plants which do not do too well in direct sunshine are the gasterias and haworthias. These turn very red or bronzed and may cease to grow in too much sunshine. In their native habitats they do not grow in the hot, dry season. It is only when the rains come that they make any new growth and flower. It is probable that in some regions where many succulents grow there may be no rainfall for a year or two. Some types of succulents grow among coarse grasses or low shrubs, where they get a certain amount of shade.

If the natural conditions of their native habitats are understood it will be easier to provide the necessary treatment for the successful growth of succulents. However, although these plants grow in so many different climatic regions, and in spite of the special treatment required by some types, it is possible to grow most kinds quite successfully by the same method of treatment, and in the same soils.

Soil and compost Most succulents are not at all particular as to the type of soil they are grown in provided it is porous. Many can be grown in almost pure sand, while some grow better in a fairly rich compost as long as the surplus water can drain away fairly quickly.

It is sometimes recommended that a special soil is used for each genus, but it is possible to grow a varied collection by using one soil only. If you have a large number of plants to pot up, you will no doubt like to mix your own soil, but where a few plants only are to be dealt with it is far easier to buy

Above, left: Aeonium palmense in its native habitat, the Canary Isles. The rosettes grow slightly inclined, to prevent moisture lodging within them.
Above, right: Brachystelma barberiae should be grown with the top half of the tuber exposed to prevent rotting.
Right: Stone chipping help drainage.

a reliable potting compost and add a little extra roughage to make up a suitable compost, or make your own as given previously for cacti.

The standard commercial potting composts have a larger proportion of loam and peat to sand than has the mixture recommended previously. Although this is excellent for ordinary plants it will be found that it holds too much moisture to be suitable for the succulents. Some need a more porous soil than others, but by adding the necessary roughage, such as grit, broken brick or charcoal, it is possible to use commercial composts for all types.

By adding the extra roughage the proportion of fertilisers will be lessened; but few succulents require a rich compost. If a compost is used which is too rich in added fertilisers it is probable that the plants will grow out of character. They may then become soft and sappy and succumb to cold, wintry conditions.

Repotting The time for repotting succulents depends on the type. As with the cacti, other kinds that have a resting period should not be repotted until growth has begun. Normally March would be the time for this task but the genus may be resting then and so must wait for a few months before being repotted. Most succulents will probably benefit from a repotting at least every two years. Any plant in a small pot which is watered occasionally will have used up most of the nourishment in the soil and so will need a change. Some of those that grow more rapidly can be repotted once a year. If the plant growth reaches the side of the pot a larger pot is needed. It is important to be able to inspect the actual soil in the pot to make certain whether the plant needs watering. All the old soil must be discarded. A good crock should almost cover the drainage hole of the pot, the larger it is the easier it will be to remove the plant when repotting again becomes necessary. The compost should be crumbly moist when potting is done, and then, as with cacti, no water need be given for a week or so.

Watering Once watering is begun in the early part of the year enough should be given each time to ensure that all the soil in the pot is well damped. It may be necessary to go over all plants again to ensure that enough has been given.

The secret of watering all succulents is to refrain from giving any more water until the soil has dried out. Remember succulents will not survive for long in a water-logged soil, so adequate drainage is essential.

Propagation Some succulents can be raised from seed and soon make sizable plants, others can be propagated by division or by taking cuttings. Many of the succulent-leaved types can be increased by taking off the leaves and rooting them in sharp sand. Where this is done the leaves should be just laid on the surface of the sand. If leaves or cuttings are pushed into the sand too deeply rot may set in causing failure to root.

1

2   4   6

3   5

Summer and winter treatment Some of the succulents which do not like excessive summer heat in the greenhouse may be placed out of doors from June to early September. They must be protected from slugs, etc. Water them occasionally during dry weather. If these plants are bedded out for the summer it will be difficult to repot them into the same sized pot when they will be removed.

Most succulents can be kept at 40-45°F (4-7°C) through the winter provided the soil is dry and they can stand any temperature they are likely to encounter during the summer.

Miniature succulent gardens Cacti and other succulents are very suitable for miniature gardens. For impact, they will depend mainly on dwarf plants, some of which may be miniature replicas of their taller counterparts while others will display their own individual characteristics.

A good way of getting horticultural quarts into pint pots is to garden in sinks and troughs. Several of these plant containers, each with its separate planting scheme, can be accommodated in a minimum of space. Many a town forecourt, backyard or balcony could benefit from the inclusion of a feature of this kind.

Unfortunately, genuine stone troughs and sinks are fast becoming collectors' items and, in consequence, increasingly

A simple indoor miniature garden can be made in a clay seed-pan, using small plants from pots and is a delightful and fascinating source of interest.
1 The base of the seed pan is covered with large crocks to ensure sharp drainage, and these are covered with moss and peat to keep the compost open and porous. 2 Compost is added to about half the depth of the pan and levelled. 3 Suitable stones, not too large and not too small, are put in position and firmed in place with a dibber. 4 and 5 Small plants are put into position and planted with a small trowel. 6 The finished garden is permanent.

Above: Small succulents have been planted in a 50mm (2 inch) shell to make a really miniature garden. Many unusual containers can be used to display succulents in this way.

difficult and expensive to come by. The stone sinks of Victorian kitchens and sculleries have long ago been replaced by vitreous enamel and stainless steel, while the larger troughs, formerly used for watering cattle and horses, have given place to galvanised iron tanks.

The occasional specimen still turns up at country sales and in junk yards, but dealers are aware of their value and prices have risen astronomically. As an alternative, concrete or old glazed sinks can be adapted for the purpose. But neither of these will have the charm of the genuine article which, if it has been out-of-doors for any length of time, will be weathered and decorated with mosses and lichens.

Particular attention must be paid to drainage before planting up any of these containers. A piece of perforated zinc should cover the existing drainage hole and the base of the trough or sink should be covered with broken crocks or stone chippings to a depth of 2-3 inches. On top of this goes a layer of peat moss or chopped turves, the latter grass side down.

The planting mixture should consist of the same compost as given for repotting. Only half fill, then when the plants are in position the rest of the soil may be added and firmed. If the soil under a flat stone, pressed into the top of the soil, is damp do not water.

Cacti for collectors

Aporocactus

From the Greek *aporos*, impenetrable, but for no obvious reason *(Cactaceae)*. Greenhouse plants with drooping, spine-covered stems up to 2 feet long. *A. flagelliformis* is the well-known 'rat-tailed cactus', suitable for window culture and hanging baskets.

Species cultivated *A. flagelliformis*, rat-tailed cactus, slender stems with fine spines, cerise-pink flowers in spring, Peru. *A. martianus*, stems erect or sprawling, flowers red to scarlet with violet edge, Mexico. *A. x mallisonii*, hybrid between *A. flagelliformis* and *Heliocereus speciosus*, large bright red flowers.

Cultivation A suitable growing medium is an average potting compost to which should be added a fifth part of sharp, coarse sand with broken brick included. Repot every two or three years, give light stimulants when in bud; give plenty of light at all times and sun whenever possible. These plants can take more water than many cacti but soil must be well drained. Temperature minimum 40°F (4°C) in winter when plants must be kept dry, 70°F (21°C) in summer.

Propagation is by seeds sown in sandy soil in spring; cover them by their own depth only and keep them moist and warm. Cuttings of young shoots may also be used for propagation, dry these before placing them on sharp sand and peat in equal quantities; do not push cuttings into this or they may rot; aerial roots often form on the stems.

Ariocarpus

From *aria*, the name for the whitebeam, and the Greek *carpos*, a fruit, referring to the shape of the fruits *(Cactaceae)*. Greenhouse cacti mainly Mexican in origin. Plants have a stout root stock, rather flat stems with no spines, the areoles are borne on tubercles. Plants have a rock-like appearance.

Species cultivated *A. fissuratus*, very rock-like, tubercles greyish and flattened, flowers pink with a darker mid-rib, south-west Texas and Mexico. *A. retusus*, flattish growth, grey tubercles flowers pale pink, Mexico. *A. trigonus*, tubercles more erect than other species, the yellowish flowers appear from the woolly top of the plant, Mexico. *A.*

kotchubeyanus, dark green tubercles with a woolly furrow, flowers pink to carmine-red, Central Mexico.

Cultivation The compost should be very porous; regular compost, with a ¼ part of added coarse sand and broken brick is suitable. Plants should be given a very sunny place in the greenhouse. Repot every four years as plants are very slow growing. Water sparingly from April to September, then give no water at all in winter. Maintain a temperature from March to September, of 70-75°F (21-24°C); plants can stand a minimum of 40°F (4°C) in winter.

Propagation is by seeds sown in spring in deep pans of a good seed compost.

Keep moist and at a temperature of 70°F (21°C) during germination. Seedlings grow very slowly; maintain warmth but give no direct sun for the first year.

Astrophytum

From the Greek *aster*, star, *phytos*, plant, referring to the shape of the plant *(Cactaceae)*. Star cactus. Formerly included in *Echinocactus*, these cacti mostly have globular stems, some deeply ridged with from four to eight ribs. Flowers are produced from areoles at the top of the plant. A well-grown specimen produces flowers at each areole as formed. There are four species and many cultivars produced through crossing.

Top: Aporocactus flagelliformis, the Rat-tailed Cactus, an easily-flowered cactus for a sunny window-sill.
Right: Ariocarpus trigonus, a spineless cactus from Mexico, with yellowish flowers.

Species cultivated *A. asterias*, round and almost ribless, flowers yellow, large, with red centre. *A. capricorne*, ribbed with strong, curved spines, flowers yellow. *A. myriostigma*, bishop's cap, spineless, flowers yellow. *A. ornatum*, many curling spines, flowers lemon-yellow. All these are natives of Mexico.

Cultivation Astrophytums should be given a very porous soil with added lime A suitable compost consists of 2 parts of loam, 1 part of peat and 1 part of sharp, coarse sand. Add 1 ounce of ground chalk and ¼ pound of reliable base fertilizer to each bushel. Repot only every four years except seedlings which may be re-potted every year. Water from April to September, after which the soil is kept quite dry; never allow soil to remain wet for long periods or the plant will rot. Give as much sun as possible at all times; there is no limit to warmth these plants can stand in summer. The temperature in winter should not fall below 40°F (4°C) As these plants never produce off-sets normally they must be grown from seed. The seeds are large with a hollow side like a cowrie shell. Sow them in a good seed compost, just pressing the seed in. They may germinate in 48 hours at a temperature of 70°F (21°C). Prick out when the cotyledon (seed-leaf) has been absorbed.

Borzicactus

Named in honour of Professor Antonio Borzi, an Italian botanist (Cactaceae). Cacti with stems often erect, but a few spreading, many ribs which are closely covered with areoles and spines, flowers round and small.

Species cultivated *B. faustianus*, pale green stem about 2 inches thick, many long spines, some yellow, flowers red, Andes of Peru. *B. fieldianus*, stems long, erect or semi-prostrate, many whitish spines, flowers red, Peru. *B. morley-anus*, long stems branching from base, slender, brownish spines, flowers carmine-violet, Ecuador.

Cultivation A compost with few additions is suitable, with added coarse matter to increase porosity; a sixth part will do. Repot in March, not more often than every two years. Water when the soil dries out in summer, but give none at all in winter. Temperature, 65-75°F (18-24°C) in summer, 40°F (4°C) in winter, when plants must be kept dry. These cacti like plenty of sun in the growing period.

Propagation is by seed sown in a good seed compost in a temperature of 70°F (21°C). Shade the seedlings for the first year. Some species may be increased by cuttings. These should be dried and placed on sharp sand to root.

Cephalocereus

From the Greek *kephale*, a head, and *Cereus*, another genus in which these plants were once placed (Cactaceae). These plants grow very tall in their

Above: Astrophytum myriostigma is called Bishop's Cap because of its shape.

natural state and sometimes branch when old. Most are ribbed with hair or wool at the areole and at the point where flowers are produced. This develops a cephalium, a thick bunch of wool, which protects the flower bud from the sun. The flowers are mostly small and narrow, almost tube-shaped. There are about 50 species and several are favourite plants with collectors as their white spines and hairs make them particularly attractive.

Species cultivated *C. aurisetus*, thick stems up to 4 feet high, branching from base, with golden-yellow bristle-like spines, cephalium on one side of stem where flowers are produced, flowers bell-shaped, yellow to white, Brazil. *C. chrysacanthus*, columnar stem up to 15 feet, glossy-green with golden yellow hairs and spines, some spines brownish, flowers open at night, deep pink, Mexico. *C. palmeri*, tall, branched bluish-green stems, very woolly areoles, thick cephalium, spines yellow when young, turning to black with age, flowers nocturnal, reddish-green with pink inside, eastern Mexico. *C. senilis*, the well known old man cactus, a great favourite with cactus collectors, grows tall with dense white hairs and spines, can reach 35-40 feet, in its native habitat, flowers are nocturnal and about 5 inches long, Mexico.

Cultivation The soil should be a good porous compost but plants are not particular provided the drainage is good. Repot every three years or as often as they out-grow their pot. Pots must have a large enough base to support the tall plants. Water well during hot weather, as often as the soil dries out; give no water in winter. Temperature 65-70°F (18-24°C) in summer, 40°F (4°C) in winter. Many species are easy to raise from seed but take years to reach flowering size. Sow seeds in the early part of the year in reliable seed compost, covering them very lightly. Keep the pots or pans moist warm and shaded, and prick out the seedlings when the cotyledon has become absorbed. Some species make branches which can be detached, the cut ends allowed to dry and then rooted on sharp sand. Tall plants can be beheaded. The base will sprout fresh shoots and the top can be dried and used as a cutting.

Cereus

From the Latin *cereus*, wax-like, pliant, referring to the stems (*Cactaceae*). Torch cactus. Greenhouse succulent plants. This genus has been split up into several genera, including *Acanthocereus, Arthrocereus, Bergerocactus, Binghamia, Borzicactus, Brachycereus, Browningia, Carnegia, Cephalocereus, Cleistocactus, Corryocactus, Dendrocereus, Erdisia, Escontria, Espostoa, Eulychnia, Haageocereus, Harrisia, Heliocereus, Jasminocereus, Lemaireocereus, Leocereus, Leptocereus, Lophocereus, Machaerocereus, Monvillea, Myrtillocactus, Neoabbottia, Neoraimondia, Nyctocereus, Oreocereus, Pacyycereus, Peniocereus, Rathbunia, Stetsonia, Trichocereus, Wilcoxia, Zehntnerella.*

The cereus have erect or sprawling stems, all with spines and all flowering at night. The flowers are mostly large and in many species are fragrant.

Species cultivated *C. chalybaeus,* up to 10 feet, in nature, stem columnar, a deep blue, 5–6 ribs, flowers red, white inside, Agentina. *C. hexagonus,* short-jointed, 6-angled stems, long white flowers, West Indies. *C. horridus,* 15–20 feet high in nature, stems branched, 4 ribs, flowers greenish-red, South America, *C. peruvianus,* 35 feet high in nature, a favourite in collections, ribs variable, 5–8, bluish-green to blue, straight spines, flowers brownish-green outside, white within, a form of monstrous growth is in cultivation, south east Brazil.

Cultivation A suitable soil consists of compost with few added nutrients, with a sixth part of added coarse sand or grit; broken brick may be incorporated in this. Repot in March or April every two or three years or more frequently if the plant grows too large for the pot. Water from March to October but give none in winter; temperature, 65°F (18°C) in summer, 40°F (4°C) in winter.

Propagation is by seed sown in a good seed compost in pans; cover the seeds lightly, keep moist and shaded at a temperature of 70°F (21°C). Prick out the seedlings when the cotyledon has

Below left: Cephalocereus senilis, the Old Man Cactus from Mexico, so called because of the grey bristles resembling coarse hair. This columnar cactus can reach 9m (30 feet) and produce pink flowers:
Below right: Cereus peruvianus.

been absorbed. Seedlings grow fairly quickly and will need an annual repot. The branching types may be increased by taking sideshoots as cuttings. These must be dried at the cut so that a skin forms before they are put in to sharp sand and peat in equal parts. Do not push the cutting too far into the compost but support it with a stick if it is tall. The base should just rest on the rooting medium. Pot up into the usual compost when roots form.

Chamaecereus

From the Greek *chamai*, ground, and *cereus;* the prostrate cereus (*Cactaceae*). Peanut cactus. This is a very popular cactus especially with beginners. There is one species only, with two or three varieties. This is *C. silvestrii,* of low prostrate growth, very spreading, with many stems. These are about little finger size and covered with small spines. The flowers, produced from May to July, are funnel-shaped, 2 inches long, bright red; vars. *cristata,* a cristate form; *elongata,* thinner stems, western Argentine.

Cultivation A good porous soil should be provided; this can be made up from a regular potting compost, plus a sixth part of sharp, coarse sand. Grow in a sunny position. This plant is very liable to become infested with red spider mite and a spraying with rain water every week helps to keep this pest at bay. Normal summer temperature is adequate but it should not fall below 40°F (4°C), in winter. Water when soil dries out in

spring and summer, gradually reducing watering in autumn. Keep quite dry in winter. The plant is easily increased by cuttings, which can be broken from the main plant and dried in the sun for a few days. Insert base in sharp sand and spray occasionally; pot up when roots are formed. Plants can be raised from seed but as it is so easy to increase by cuttings, seed sowing is hardly worthwhile.

Cleistocactus
From the Greek *kleistos*, closed (the flowers scarcely open) and *cactus*. Greenhouse perennial cacti (*Cactaceae*). Tall-growing cacti of the cereus group, mostly slender, many branched at times, with numerous ribs with closely set areoles and spines, flowers small with narrow tube. They are favourites with cactus collectors as they give height to groups.

Species cultivated Among fifteen species the following are likely to be found in cultivation. *C. baumannii*, upright growth, many yellow-brown spines, flowers orange-scarlet, narrow, western Argentina. *C. smaragdiflorus*, erect with long golden and brown spines, Uruguay. *C. strausii*, handsome white-spined and hairy plant, flowers red, small, can be grown as a house plant if given plenty of light, Bolivia.

Cultivation These cacti are easy to grow in John Innes potting compost No. 1, to which is added a sixth part of sharp sand or grit. Pot in large enough containers to prevent the plants from falling over, and repot when the pot is too small or every three years. Water as often as soil dries out from March to September; keep dry in winter. Keep them in a sunny place in a temperature of 65–75°F (18–24°C) in summer, 40°F (4°C) in winter. Propagation is by seed sown as for most cacti, or by cuttings of sideshoots or by beheading the plant. The top, when the cut surface is dry, soon forms roots, and the old plant will make new shoots where it has been cut, to provide further cuttings.

Coryphantha
From the Greek *koryphe*, top, *anthas*, a flower, since the flowers appear from the top of the plant (*Cactaceae*). Greenhouse cacti, first introduced into this country in the seventeenth century, which can be identified by the stout spines usually in a group on an areole and shaped like a spider.

Species cultivated *C. andreae*, large yellow flowers. *C. asterias*, globular to columnar, flowers pinkish-white. *C. bumamma*, thick tubercles, yellow flowers. *C. clava*, taller growing, with yellow flowers. *C. elephantidens*, very thick, short tubercles, flowers large, pinkish-red. All from Mexico.

Cultivation Pot every three years in a regular potting compost, with a sixth part added of sharp sand, grit

Top: Chamaecereus silvestrii, a prostrate plant from Argentina; the only species in this genus and sometimes called the peanut cactus. Propagation is by means of short branches which are easily detached and readily root in a sandy compost.
Above: Coryphantha bonantii, a cactus in the sub-tribe that includes the Mammillarias.

and broken brick. Position in full sun on a shelf in the greenhouse, give air on all suitable occasions, water March to September and spray in the evening after a hot day. Some types with tap roots require very deep pots. They are not as free flowering as many cacti.

Temperatures in summer should range from 65–75°F (18–21°C), with a winter minimum of 40°F (4°C). Propagation is by seed sown in a good seed compost in early spring, covering the seeds very lightly only. Keep them moist, at 70°F (21°C) and shade the seedlings from sunshine for the first year. Some species make offsets which can be detached and rooted, or tops can be cut from plants, the cut surfaces dried and then rooted.

Dolichothele
From the Greek *dolikos*, long, *thele*, nipple, referring to the long tubercles (*Cactaceae*). Greenhouse cactus plants, recognisable by their large fleshy tubercles; all have large yellow flowers followed by greenish fruits. The roots become very thick and parsnip-like.

Species cultivated *D. longimamma*, thick tap root, stout tubercles, stem bright green with areole on top with several spines, central Mexico. *D. melaleuca*, rather shorter tubercles, otherwise similar, flowers with reddish tips to the petals, Mexico. *D. uberiformis*, stout tubercles, free-flowering, Mexico.

Cultivation Pot in a regular potting compost with added sharp sand, grit and broken brick, at the rate of a sixth part; repot when the plant reaches the side of the pot or every two or three years. Place the pots on the greenhouse shelf in sunshine. Water from April to September, gradually reduce to none at all from October to March. Temperature, any summer warmth and a minimum of 40°F (4°C), in winter when the plants are kept dry. Propagation is by seed sown in a good seed compost, just covering the seed with its own depth of soil, in a temperature of 70°F (21°C). Keep the seedlings moist and shaded from sun.

Echinocactus
From the Greek *echinos*, a hedgehog, and *Cactus*, referring to the numerous spines (*Cactaceae*). Greenhouse cactus plants. Many new genera have been formed from this genus, including: *Astrophytum*, *Epithelantha*, *Ferocactus*, *Gymnocalycium*, *Hamatacactus*, *Malacocarpus*, *Notocactus*, and *Parodia*. Most species are large growing and are not easy to flower in temperate climates owing to the lack of strong sunshine.

Species cultivated *E. ingens*, stem globular becoming columnar when old, greenish-grey, woolly at the top, ribs increasing in number with age, flowers reddish-yellow. *E. grusonii*, golden barrel cactus, mother-in-law's chair, a great favourite, a football-shaped plant with many strong, golden-yellow spines. It is not likely to flower in Britain. *E. visnaga*, large-growing species, flowers glossy yellow. All are from Mexico.

Cultivation The medium should consist of compost with few added nutrients with a sixth part extra of sharp sand, grit and broken brick in well-drained

Three Mexican cacti: Above left, Echinocactus grusonii rarely flowers in the north. Above right, Echinocereus reichenbachii, a Hedgehog Cactus from Texas and Mexico. Left, Echinocereus blanckii, will withstand cold if kept dry.

pots. The plants should be given a position in a sunny greenhouse. Repot every three or four years or when the plant reaches the side of its pot. Water sparingly from March to September; keep quite dry in winter. Temperatures: 65–75°F (18–24°C) in summer and 40°F (4°C) in winter. Give plenty of ventilation in hot weather. As these plants rarely make offsets propagation is from seed sown in a good seed compost. Just cover the seed lightly, keep moist and shaded in a temperature of 70°F (21°C).

Echinocereus

From the Greek *echinos*, a hedgehog, and *Cereus*, referring to the very prickly nature of the plants (*Cactaceae*). Greenhouse cacti, first introduced in the late seventeenth century; a large genus with erect and spreading stems and mostly with large and spectacular flowers.

Species cultivated *E. berlandieri*, thick sprawling stems with strong spines, flowers large, pink, Mexico. *E. blanckii*, stems sprawling, flowers purple, Mexico and Texas. *E. dubius*, stems yellowish-green, fleshy, flowers pink, south-east Texas. *E. reichenbachii* (syn. *E. caespitosus*), stems stiff, erect, with numerous yellowish spines, flowers pinkish-purple, Mexico, Texas, *E. rigidissimus*, the popular rainbow cactus, stem erect, stout with many ribs closely covered with short spines, which are coloured reddish near the top of plant, flowers pink, Mexico and Arizona. Almost all shades of colour are to be found in this genus.

Cultivation A suitable medium is an average potting compost, with a sixth part extra of grit, coarse sand and broken brick. Grow the plants on a sunny shelf in the greenhouse. Pot every two years for adult plants, every year for young seedling plants. Water the plants when the soil dries out from March to September, but give no water in winter. Temperatures should be 65–75°F (18–24°C) in the growing period, 40°F (4°C) in winter. Propagation is by seeds sown in a good seed compost in early spring; keep moist and at 70°F (21°C), shaded from direct sunshine. Several species with branching habit can be increased by taking sideshoots as cuttings. Dry them well and stand them on sharp sand to root.

Echinofossulocactus

From the Greek *echinos*, a hedgehog; the Latin *fossula*, a groove, and *Cactus*, referring to the grooved, prickly plants (*Cactaceae*). Greenhouse cacti, sometimes found under the genus *Stenocactus*. An easily recognised genus as the plants are globular and later columnar, with many ribs, up to 35 in some species. These ribs are very thin and wavy, thus presenting plenty of skin to the atmosphere but not to the direct rays of the sun. The flowers are all produced at the growing tip of plant.

Species cultivated *E. crispatus*, about 25 ribs, with strong spines, purple flowers. *E. hastatus*, 35 wavy ribs, stiff spines, flowers yellowish-white. *E. xiphacanthus*, very strong flattened, sword-like spines, flowers pale mauve. All are from Mexico.

Cultivation The compost should be very porous, made from a compost with few added nutrients, plus a sixth part of sharp sand, grit and broken brick added. Use a pot just larger than the base of the plant. Repot in March or April, water sparingly at all times and give none in winter. Temperatures should range from 65–80°F (18–27°C) in summer, down to 40°F (4°C) in winter. Plants like plenty of sunshine. Propagation is by seed sown in a good seed compost in pans in early spring in a temperature of 70°F (21°C). Shade the seedlings from sun while young. Few plants make offsets.

Echinopsis

From the Greek *echinos*, a hedgehog, *opsis*, like; the spiny plants resemble a rolled-up hedgehog (*Cactaceae*). Hedgehog cactus. Greenhouse cacti, first introduced in the early nineteenth century, among the commonest cactus plants in cultivation. They are globular when young, columnar with age. They have several deep ridges or ribs with areoles and stiff spines; their large, often fragrant flowers open for about 36 hours.

Species cultivated *E. eyriesii*, to 6 inches tall, 11–18 ribs, flowers white, fragrant, Mexico. *E. leucantha*, 14 ribs, strong spines, flowers brownish-green outside, inside white, Chile, western Argentina. *E. multiplex*, makes many offsets, pale green body, ribs 13–15, flowers pink, fragrant, southern Brazil. *E. tubiflora*, globular when young, columnar with age up to 18 inches in height, flower a long tube, white to pink, brown on the outside, southern Brazil.

Cultivation The compost should be made up from an average potting compost with a sixth part of coarse sand, grit and broken brick added, in well-drained pots. Give the plants a sunny place in a window or greenhouse. Repot every two or three years. Some species flower better if their offsets are removed. Temperatures: March to September, 65–75°F (18–24°C), September to March, 40–45°F (4–7°C). Propagation is by rooting offsets which are usually freely produced; some form roots while still attached to the parent plant. New kinds are raised from seed when offsets are not available; sow

Above: Echinofossulocactus lamellosus, a many-ribbed Mexican cactus, produces red flowers on a short tube.

in a good seed compost, in a temperature of 70°F (21°C); keep the seedlings moist and shaded and prick them off when large enough to handle and the cotyledon has been absorbed.

Epiphyllum

From the Greek *epi*, upon, *phyllon*, a leaf; the flowers are produced on the leaf-like branches (*Cactaceae*). Succulent greenhouse plants, epiphytic cacti, previously known as *Phyllocactus*, introduced in the early nineteenth century when they became very popular in stovehouses. Many now in cultivation are not true species but hybrids between a *Selenicereus* and a *Nopalxochia*.

Species cultivated *E. anguliger*, bushy growth with erect stems, well notched, very few spines at areoles, flowers tubular, scented, greenish-yellow outside and white inside, southern Mexico. *E. crenatum*, branches thick and notched, to 3 feet high, flowers greenish-yellow to white. Guatemala. *E. oxype-*

talum, branches thin and long, flowers reddish on outer petals, white inside, Brazil and Mexico. The hybrid type usually found under the name of *E.* × *ackermannii* is the one often grown as a house plant and flowers every year, if grown under good conditions, especially in a sunny window. There are hundreds of named varieties of this hybrid, with very large flowers in a wide range of colours.

Cultivation These plants are easily grown and will thrive in almost any type of compost. The best results, however, are obtained in a rich soil composed of 6 parts of loam, 2 parts of peat and 2 parts of sharp sand. Repot plants when they become potbound, water them freely from April to September. Keep them in the greenhouse in winter and spring, but place them out of doors for summer. Plants do not like too strong sunshine in an unshaded greenhouse. Propagation is by seeds sown as for cacti, or by cuttings. These are easily obtained from young shoots, even a section of a shoot will make roots if dried at the cut part first. Root in sharp sand.

Ferocactus

From the Latin *ferus*, wild, and *cactus;* the plants are very spiny (*Cactaceae*). Hedgehog cactus. A genus of greenhouse cacti, globular plants, becoming columnar with age, with thick prominent ribs armed with strong spines, some hooked.

Species cultivated *F. latispinus*, stem globular, depressed at top, the areoles with a group of strong, curved spines, flowers funnel-shaped, carmine-red, Mexico. *F. pringlei*, sometimes branches from base, flowers red-orange, yellow inside, central Mexico. *F. wislizenii*, globular when young, growing to 6 feet high in its native habitat, 15–20 ribs, spines thick and strong, some hooked, flowers reddish-yellow, Texas.

Cultivation These cacti thrive in a compost consisting of a regular potting compost with a sixth part of extra sand grit or broken brick. They should be given a sunny position in the greenhouse. Repot every two or three years in March. Water from March to September, only when the soil has completely dried out. Temperature: 65–75°F (18–24°C), March to September, 40°F (4°C), September to March, when the soil must be kept dry. Propagation is by seed sown in pans of reliable seed compost, when a temperature of 70°F (21°C), can be maintained; just cover the seed and keep moist and shaded. These plants do not normally make offsets unless the top is cut off. This can be dried and rooted, the base will then produce offsets.

Gymnocalycium

From the Greek *gymnos*, naked, *kalyx*, bud; the flower buds having no covering (*Cactaceae*). Greenhouse cacti, mostly single-stemmed but a few species making offsets. All have shallow ribs with a 'chin' below the areole, and the majority are not heavily spined. The flowers are

Top left: Epiphyllums produce their flowers on leaf-like branches.
Top right: Epiphyllum 'Niobe', a hybrid easily grown and propagated by cuttings.
Above: Ferocactus acanthodes, a round-ribbed plant from North Western America. It has long, bristle-like red spines.

large for the size of plant. Flower colours are variable, pink or white occurring on normally red or yellow flowered species.
Species cultivated *G. andreae*, flattened

globular, fine spines, flowers yellow, Argentina. *G. bodenbenderianum*, flattish growth, brownish-green, young spines almost black, flowers white, pink flushed. Argentina. *G. bruchii*, smallest of the gymnocalyciums, freely clustering, very weak spines, flowers white, Argentina. *G. damsii*, broad ribs, dark red markings below chins, flowers white, North Paraguay.

Cultivation A potting compost with few added nutrients plus a sixth part of sharp sand, grit and broken brick. Keep the plants on a sunny shelf in the greenhouse, water from March to September, gradually decrease in October, then keep dry all winter. Temperatures should be 65–75°F (18–24°C) during the growing period, 40–45°F (4–7°C) in winter. Propagation is by seed sown in pans of a good seed compost in early spring. Keep moist and shaded in a temperature of 70°F (21°C). Offsets may be rooted from species which develop them.

Harrisia

Commemorating William Harris, Superintendent of the Public Gardens, Jamaica (*Cactaceae*). A genus of tall-growing greenhouse succulents, erect when young, becoming sprawling when older. The stems are narrow with few groups of spines. The flowers are mostly white, nocturnal and fragrant. Some species are used as grafting stock.
Species cultivated *H. bonplandii*, stem tortuous with few strong spines, flowers large, white, followed by red plum-like fruits, Brazil. *H. guelichii*, pale green stems young spines, reddish later turning grey, flowers green and white Brazil, *H. martinii*, stems several feet long, few spines, flower white, Argentina. *H. jusbertii*, stems mostly erect, branching later, flowers white inside,

Right: The pink flowers of Gymnocalycium mostii, an Argentinian species.
Far right: The satiny-yellow flowers of Gymnocalycium andreae, also from Argentina.
Below: The stems of Harrisia guelichii bear spines which are reddish when young.

brownish outside, Paraguay.
Cultivation A compost consisting of a rich potting compost with a sixth part added of roughage composed of sharp sand, grit and broken brick, is suitable. Repot every two or three years in March. Water March to September as often as the soil dries out; keep dry from October to March. Grow in a sunny greenhouse and support the growths with a frame or a stick when tall. Propagation is by seed sown in a good seed compost in early spring. Shade and keep moist in a temperature of 70°F (21°C). Cuttings may also be made from side shoots, dried and rooted in sharp sand.

Hylocereus

From the Greek *hyle*, wood and *Cereus;* the plants are found in forests (*Cactaceae*). A genus of epiphytic cacti, with three-angled or winged stems, often forming aerial roots. The flowers are large and open at night.
Species cultivated *H. antiguensis*, stems three-angled, few spines, flowers greenish-white to yellow, Antigua. *H. calcaratus*, climbing type with winged joints, flowers cream, Costa Rica. *H. lemairei*, tall growing, needs support, flowers long, yellowish-green, tipped red, West Indies. *H. monacanthus*, stems triangular, flowers white with outer

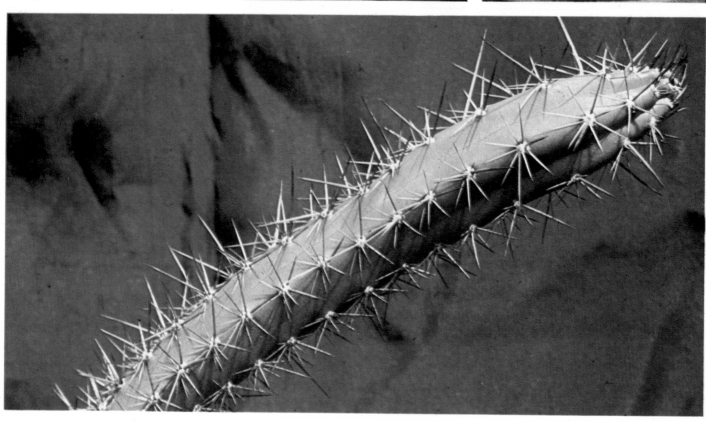

petals greenish-yellow, Colombia. *H. undatus*, thick green stem, useful as a stock for grafting cacti, sometimes found under the name of *Cereus triangularis*, flowers large, yellow to purple outside, white inside, Central America.

Cultivation Provide a compost consisting of rich potting compost with added roughage, a sixth part of sand, grit and broken brick. The addition of leafmould is advantageous. Repot every other year in March. Plants must be trained over the roof of the greenhouse or on frames. Water when dry from March to September, give a little water in winter provided plants are kept warm. Temperatures: 65–75°F (18–21°C) in the growing period, 55–60°F (13–16°C) in winter. Provide shade from strong sun. Propagation is by seed sown as for cacti or by cuttings taken from May to July, dried and rooted in sharp sand and peat, in equal parts.

Lemaireocereus

Commemorating Charles Lemaire, 1801–71, a famous French cactus specialist (*Cactaceae*). A genus of some 23 species of greenhouse succulent plants, mostly from South America, with generally erect stems, and large areoles with strong spines. They are day flowering, the flowers rather large, with short petals. This is a very good genus for increasing the height of a cactus collection. All the species described below are from Mexico.

Species cultivated *L. chende*, deep green branches from the base, small white flowers with pale pink midrib. *L. chichipe*, small plant, reddish spines, white bloom on stem, small flowers, brown-red, and greenish-yellow on inside. *L. dumortieri*, very prominent ribs, 5–6 funnel-shaped flowers, brownish-white, and reddish outside. *L. hollianos*, much branched from the base, slender spines, white flowers. *L. marginatus*, often used for hedging purposes in Mexico, grey-brown areoles, almost continuous down the edges of the ribs, handsome, bell-shaped, red and greenish-white flowers. *L. pruinosus*, stem blue when young, flowers funnel-shaped, brownish-green to white.

Cultivation An average potting compost with $\frac{1}{6}$ part extra of sand, grit and broken brick to add to the porosity is the best for these plants; repotting is done every three years, or sooner if pot-bound. Place in a really sunny position in the greenhouse—on tall plants flowering will only take place in full sun. They should be watered between March and September, and kept quite dry for the rest of the year. During winter the temperature should be 55°F (13°C), but in summer any greenhouse temperature will do with plenty of ventilation. Propagate by seed sown in John Innes seed compost, just covered, and kept at a temperature of 70–80°F (21–27°C), moist,

and shaded for the first year. Seedlings are fairly quick growing. Propagate also from side-shoots removed and used as cuttings; when these are dry they soon root in sand.

Leuchtenbergia

Commemorating Eugene de Beauharnais, Duke of Leuchtenberg, 1781–1824, a

French soldier and statesman (*Cactaceae*). A peculiar cactus from Central and North Mexico with stout, parsnip-like roots. It appears to have many leaves coming from a central stem; these are not leaves, however, but well-developed tubercles. On top of each is the areole with a cluster of long papery spines. One species only is cultivated *L. principis*, the flowers of which come from the top of the central tubercles. They are funnel-shaped, yellow and reddish-brown.

Cultivation A compost with few added nutrients with $\frac{1}{6}$ part added of sand, grit and broken brick is suitable. A little extra ground chalk can be added, about 1 ounce per bushel. Repot in March every 3 years, or before if pot bound, using deep pots. Place in full sun in the greenhouse, and do not water often, only when the soil is dry, between April and September, and keep quite dry in winter. The winter minimum temperature should be 40°F (4°C), in summer ordinary greenhouse temperature, provided there is plenty of ventilation. Propagate by seed sown in a regular seed compost in pans in March. Keep them at 70°F (21°C),

Left: The large yellow flower of Hylocereus undatus, a central American cactus.
Below: Hylocereus is an epiphytic cactus.

moist and shaded until the seedlings appear. Plants may also be propagated by rooting tubercles in sand.

Lobivia

The name is an anagram of Bolivia, where the plants are found (*Cactaceae*). A genus of greenhouse succulents, mostly dwarf and cylindrical with large and colourful flowers of the size of the plant.

Species cultivated *L. aurea*, globular to columnar ridged stems, yellow flowers. *L. backebergii*, a handsome plant with carmine flowers. *L. famatimensis*, yellow to red; vars. *albiflora*, white or pale yellow; *aurantiaca*, golden-orange; *haematantha*, blood-red; *rosiflora*, pink. *L. hertrichiana*, small globular bodies, few spines, bright red flowers, produces offsets very freely. *L. jajoiana*, very handsome, dark red flowers with black centre.

Cultivation Use an average potting compost with $\frac{1}{6}$ part extra of sand, grit and broken brick. Plants should be re-potted every two years and given a very sunny position. Water between March and September, but keep very dry in winter.

Below left: Lemaireocereus chichipe, from Mexico.
Right: Leuchtenbergia principis, a Mexican cactus. What appear to be leaves are, in fact, well developed tubercles.
Bottom right: The yellow flower of L. principis.

The summer temperature can be between 65°F (18°C) and 85°F (30°C); winter temperature should not drop below 40°F (4°C). Propagate by seed sown in a good seed compost, just covered, and kept close in a temperature of 70°F (25°C). Plants may also be propagated from offsets rooted in coarse sand.

Lophocereus

From the Greek *lophos*, a crest, and *cereus*, referring to the bristly top of the flowering stem (*Cactaceae*). There is one species only in this genus, *L. schottii*, from Arizona, a tall cactus with thick stems with short, strong spines. A few offsets are produced at the base of the plant. Flowering areoles develop long

broken brick. They require re-potting every three or four years, and the sunniest position in the greenhouse. Do not water between October and March, and in the remaining time, only when the soil has dried out. Temperature in the winter should be 40°F (4°C) minimum, but the normal seasonal summer temperature will be satisfactory. Plants tend to shrink and become very soft in winter, but quickly firm up when watered. Propagate from seed sown in a good seed compost and lightly covered. Keep shaded and moist at a temperature of 75°F (24°C). The plants make offsets when older, but these are difficult to remove for cuttings.

Mammillaria

From the Latin *mamma*, the breast, or *mamilla*, nipple, in reference to the teat-like tubercles of many species (*Cactaceae*). A large genus of greenhouse succulent perennials, suitable for window culture. Most species are from the southern parts of North America and Mexico and can be recognised by the numerous tubercles covering them; there are no ribs as on many globular cacti. They are mostly dwarf plants forming large groups (*caespitose*), but there are a few taller ones. Mammillarias have areoles between the tubercles from which flowers arise; they also have areoles on the tops of the tubercles from which the species arise. Offsets can form from either type of areole. The flowers are produced in rings near the growing centre between the tubercles (axils). No more flowers will appear at the areole where it has already borne a flower and so fresh growth must be encouraged each year.

Species cultivated There are over 300 species and many varieties—the following is a mere selection: *M. albicans*, densely covered with white spines, red flowers. *M. bocasana*, grouping, with silky white hairs and red hooks, flowers pink. *M. camptotricha*, pale green body with golden twisting spines, white flowers. *M. decipiens*, grouping, large tubercles with red spines, flowers pink or white. *M. elongata*, finger-like stems, many varieties, flowers white. *M. fraileana*, tall-growing with strong hooks, large pink flowers. *M. gracilis*, small type with offsets which fall readily, flowers yellowish. *M. hahniana*, very attractive, with long white hairs, red flowers, *M. innae*, small-growing, white-spined species, red flowers. *M. jaliscana*, globular, freely offsetting with large pinkish-red flowers. *M. karwinskiana*, open type with strong spines, cream coloured inner petals. *M. longiflora*, very long thin tubercles, many thin spines, long tubed pink flowers, central spine hooked. *M. magnimamma*, open type with many varieties, strong spines, flowers cream. *M. nunezii*, columnar growing, many fine spines, red flowers. *M. orcuttii*, dense white wool at top with

bristles at right angles to the stem. The flowers are pale green outside, pink inside, and open at night. A monstrous form of this plant is also cultivated. This has irregular ribs and no spines. The plant has a knobbly appearance.

Cultivation The compost should consist of rich compost with ⅙ part added of coarse sand, grit or broken brick. Winter temperature should be a minimum of 45°F (7°C). In summer normal greenhouse temperatures suffice. It may be grown in either shade or full sun. Propagation is mainly by seed sown in reliable seed compost and kept moist and shaded at 70°F (21°C) until seedlings appear when more light can be given. Offsets on the tops of tall plants can be removed and rooted in a mixture of coarse sand and peat after allowing the cut surface to dry for two days.

Lophophora

From the Greek *lophos*, a crest, and *phoreo*, I bear, referring to the hairs borne on the areoles (*Cactaceae*). A small genus of greenhouse cacti from Central

Above: Lobivia carmianantha, a typical cactus plant from Bolivia.

America, previously known as *Anaholium* and once placed under *Echinocactus*. The drug called mescal or peyotl is extracted from them and was used by the ancient Mexicans in religious rites. It is supposed to give the eaters hallucinations when they hear sweet music and have pleasant dreams. Recent research has shown it to be a powerful emetic. The plants have a strong root-stock, no main ridges and no spines. Areoles are present with tufts of wool.

Species cultivated *L. lewinii*, larger-growing version of the following species, small pink flowers, summer. *L. williamsii*, plump, almost round stem, no spines, pink flowers, summer. There is a cristate form of this in cultivation. *L. zeigleri*, a single head, pale yellow flowers.

Cultivation Lophophoras grow well in compost with few added nutrients with ⅙ part added of sharp sand, grit and

dark spines, flowers pale red with darker mid-rib. *M. plumosa*, handsome species with feather-like spines, flowers pink, December. *M. quevedoi*, globular with white spines and wool at top. *M. rhodantha*, columnar growth with brassy spines, flowers pink. *M. spinosissima*, tall cylindrical type with many spines, yellow, brown, or red, flowers purplish. *M. tetracantha*, open type, with stiff spines, flowers pink. *M. uncinata*, open type with a hooked spine at each areole, flowers pink. *M. vaupelii*, covered with yellow and brown short spines, attractive. *M. wildii*, common species with yellow spines and hooks, flowers white.

Left: Mammillaria bocasana grows in groups and has silky white hairs and red hooks from the areoles all over the plant. The flowers are papery and silver-pink in colour.
Below: A group of Mammillaria geminispina.

M. xanthina, rare species with strong hooks. *M. yaquensis*, small type making groups with fierce hooks. *M. zeilmanniana*, the most free-flowering species, with soft tubercles and cerise flowers.

Cultivation Grow mammillarias in an average potting compost with $\frac{1}{6}$ part of sharp sand, grit and broken brick added. Repot in March or April, once every year or two; do not use a large pot. Water well from March to October, as often as the soil dries out, but do not give any water from October to February. The temperature in winter should be 40°F (4°C) and in summer 65–85°F (18–30°C). Some species, from Baja, California and the West Indies, require a higher winter temperature. Some open types need a little shade from strong sunshine. Plants are easily raised from seed sown in pans of a good seed compost in February in a temperature of 70°F (21°C). Keep the pans of seedlings at this temperature, moist and shaded. Offsets may also be rooted in a mixture of sharp sand and peat in equal parts. Some species may be increased by detaching and rooting tubercles.

Mammillopsis

From *Mammillaria*, and the Greek *opsis*, appearance, in reference to their resemblance to the mammillarias (*Cactaceae*). A genus of a few species of greenhouse succulent plants, with white spines. They make handsome plants not commonly found in collections. The white spines, many of which are hooked, form a dense covering.

Species cultivated *M. diguetii* has stronger spines and smaller flowers than the following species, Mexico. *M. senilis*, a very attractive plant, globular to cylindrical, with many white spines and hooks, reddish flowers 2 inches across, Mexico. Must have plenty of light and air.

Cultivation Use compost with few added nutrients with $\frac{1}{6}$ part added of coarse sandy grit and broken brick. Pot every three years in March, and give the plants a very sunny place in the greenhouse. Do not water between October and March, but between March and September water well when the soil in the pot has dried out. The winter temperature should not be less than 40°F (4°C). Propagate from seed sown in pans of regular seed compost, where a temperature of 70°F (21°C) can be maintained. Cover the seed lightly, keep it moist and shaded until germination, then give light but not direct sun. Offsets can be removed and rooted in coarse sand.

Mediolobivia

From the Latin *medius*, middle, and *Lobivia*, an anagram of Bolivia; this cactus could be said to be between *Rebutia* and *Lobivia* (*Cactaceae*). Small cacti from Argentina, for the greenhouse or for window cultivation, they have

ribs, which rebutias do not, while the flowers are similar to those of *Lobivia*, although smaller. They may still be listed under the generic name *Rebutia*.

Species cultivated *M. aureiflora*, short stem with many small spines, offsets very freely, golden-yellow flowers. *M. duursmaiana*, makes a group of plants, with slender radial spines and long central ones, tube-shaped orange-yellow flowers. *M. elegans*, globular pale green stem, tufted growth with fine short spines, bright yellow flowers with a long tube covered in hairs and scales.

Cultivation Pot in an average potting compost with ⅙ part added of sharp sand and other roughage. Repot in March every two years. They do best in a sunny position, and need to be watered as the soil dries out from April to September, but for the rest of the year should be kept dry. In winter, maintain a minimum temperature of 40°F (4°C) and 65–90°F (18–27°C) during the growing season while watering. Propagate by seed sown in a good seed compost in pans early in the year, keep it moist, shaded and at a temperature of 70°F (21°C). Most plants make offsets, but it is difficult to remove them for cuttings without damaging the plant.

Melocactus
From the Greek *melon*, the melon, and *kaktos*, spiny plant, a reference to the globular shape of this cactus (*Cactaceae*). These are greenhouse succulent perennials globular to barrel-shaped, with 9–20 ribs. The majority have short spines, but some species have spines 6 inches long. At the top of the plant a 'cephalium' forms to protect the flower buds—it is composed of matted wool or fine hair, and has given rise to the popular name turk's cap cactus. They are very tender plants.

Species cultivated *M. amoenus*, globular, with acute ribs and strong spines, small pink flowers, Colombia. *M. broadwayi*, globular to barrel-shaped, stout awl-shaped spines, small pink to pale purple flowers, West Indies. *M. maxonii*, globular, reddish spines, pink and white flowers, Guatemala. *M. townsendii*, globular, sometimes forming groups, pink flowers, Peru. *M. zuccarinii*, sometimes branches at the base, awl-shaped spines, small pink flowers, Venezuela.

Cultivation Use compost with few added nutrients with ⅙ part extra sand, grit and broken brick. They should be repotted every three or four years in March, and kept in the sunniest position

in the greenhouse. Water well during hot weather, but only when the soil has dried out, between March and September; for the rest of the year do not water at all. Some species, especially those from the West Indies, require the addition of a very small quantity of common salt to the water. During the winter the temperature should not drop below 60°F (16°C), but in the summer they will stand the highest temperatures, provided there is adequate ventilation Propagate by seed sown in a good seed compost in March, kept moist and shaded in a temperature of 75°F (24°C). They are very slow-growing, but the seedlings can be hastened by grafting them on to a *Trichocereus* stock.

Myrtillocactus
From the Greek *myrtillos*, the diminutive of the word for myrtle, in reference to the small fruit (*Cactaceae*). These are greenhouse succulent plants from the Americas, formerly included in the genus *Cereus*. They have strong, upright stems with six to eight ridges and stiff spines. Unlike most cacti, anything up to nine flowers can form each areole.

Species cultivated *M. cochal*, stems pale bluish when young, but the colour darkens with age, sometimes considered to be only a variety of *M. geometrizans*, California. *M. eichlamii*, dark green stems, areoles woolly where the flowers are produced, Guatemala. *M. geometrizans*, bluish-green stems, edible fruit, often grown as hedge, Mexico. *M. pugionifer*, very blue stems, Mexico. All have creamy-white diurnal flowers.

Cultivation A fairly rich but porous compost suits these plants best, and a suitable one would be an average potting compost with ⅙ part added of coarse sand or broken brick. Repot in April or May in pots large enough to support the plants if they grow tall. Water during spring and summer as often as the soil dries out, but keep the soil quite dry during winter, when a minimum temperature of 55°F (13°C) should be maintained. In the growing season they require a temperature of 65–80°F (18–27°C). Give them a sunny position in the greenhouse. Propagation is by seed sown in a good seed compost in pans in February-March, in a temperature of 70°F (21°C). Prick out the seedlings when they are large enough to handle. These cacti can also be propagated by offsets which can form at the base of the plant or from the top of a beheaded plant, and which are rooted, when the base is dry, in a compost of sand and peat.

Neolloydia
Commemorating Prof. F. E. Lloyd, a

Left: Mediolobivia elegans is a cactus of globular growth covered with fine hairs. The flowers are showy and orange-yellow in colour.

collector of cacti (*Cactaceae*). A genus of 8 species of greenhouse succulent plants, which make small groups and are dwarf growing. Their ribs are arranged in spirals with spiny tubercles. The spines are attractive and the flowers showy.

Species cultivated *N. beguinii*, plant often solitary when young, many ribbed and spiny flowers pinkish-violet, Mexico. *N. ceratites*, oval, greyish-green stem, many greyish-white spines, flowers purple, Mexico. *N. conoidea*, plant has been included in *Echinocactus*, *Mammillaria* and *Coryphantha* at various times; handsome plant with violet to red flowers Texas. *N. grandiflora*, cylindrical stem with short wartlike tubercles, often woolly, flowers large, deep violet-pink, Tamaulipas, Mexico. *N. texensis*, considered to be a form of *N. conoidea*, N. Texas.

Cultivation As for most cacti a porous soil is essential. A suitable medium is an average potting compost, with ⅕ part added of coarse sand and broken brick. Repot every two or three years in medium-sized pots. Keep the plants in a sunny place in greenhouse. Water from March to September, as often as the soil dries out. Rest the plants during winter, keeping the soil dry. The usual greenhouse temperatures are adequate in summer, in winter maintain a minimum temperature of 40°F (4°C). Propagation is by seed sown on a good seed compost. Do not cover the seed but just press it in to the compost. Keep the pans in a temperature of 70°F (21°C), and shade them from sun. February or March are the best sowing times. Prick the seedlings out after six months; rather slow growing. Plants may also be propagated by cuttings taken from divided plants or sideshoots.

Nopalea

From the Mexican name for some of the Opuntias (*Cactaceae*). A genus of about 8 species of greenhouse succulent plants, formerly included in the genus *Opuntia*, natives of Mexico and Guatemala. The plants grow tall and become tree-like. They carry small leaves on new growth which soon fall. They bear few glochids on the areoles.

Species cultivated *N. auberi*, tree-like growth up to 25 feet, joints long and narrow, flowers pink, Mexico. *N. coccinellifera*, to 12 feet high, oval joints, rather long, flowers bright red, tropical Mexico. This was used as the host plant for raising the cochineal insect from which the red dye used in food is extracted. *N. dejecta*, forms a shrub about 6 feet high, straggling growth, flowers red, south Mexico. *N. kerwinskiana*, tree-like, with long joints, flowers large, reddish pink.

Cultivation A suitable medium consists of an average potting compost, with

Right: Nopalea, a cactus from Mexico is closely related to the Opuntias.

added roughage made up of coarse sand, broken brick and granulated charcoal. Repot the plants every two years in spring. Water from March to October as often as the soil dries out. Keep the pots on a sunny shelf in the greenhouse. These cacti enjoy more warmth than opuntias, so the summer temperatures should be between 65° and 85°F(18–29°C). In winter water very sparingly, just enough to prevent the plants from shrinking, and maintain a temperature not below 45°F (7°C). Propagation is by seed sown in John Innes seed compost in early spring. Just cover the seed. Prick out the seedlings when they are an inch high. Or plants may be propagated by cuttings of pads which are freely produced. Dry the base of the pad and set it on a mixture of sharp sand and peat in equal parts. Support the cutting with a stick until it has rooted as the base should not be buried in the mixture.

Nopalxochia

From the Aztec name (*Cactaceae*). A genus of 3 species of greenhouse succulent plants, natives of Mexico southwards to Peru. One species only is in cultivation. This is suitable for window culture. *N. phyllanthoides* is an epiphyte from Mexico and Colombia, which grows bushy and erect, up to 3 feet tall, with many branches or stems which are flat and usually rounded at the base. The flowers, borne in spring, have a long tube with many stamens. They are pink or red and are produced freely. There are many hybrids with flowers in red, pink, purple and orange. The plant has been used as a parent plant for the many hybrid epiphyllums grown in collections today.

Cultivation An average potting compost with added leafmould is a suitable soil mixture. Repot annually in well-drained pots. When buds appear give liquid feeds every two weeks. The plant does not require strong sunshine and is better placed out of the greenhouse from June to September. Water well from March to September but keep the soil fairly dry during winter, although a little water can be given once a month. Maintain a winter temperature of 45°F (7°C), rising in summer to 65°F (18°C). Propagation is from seed as for other cacti or by cuttings which are freely produced. Dry the cut surface and root the cuttings in sharp sand and peat in equal parts. Keep them shaded and spray them occasionally while they are taking root.

Notocactus

From the Greek *notos*, south, and *cactus*, but for obscure reasons (*Cactaceae*). A genus of 15 species of greenhouse succulent perennials, from subtropical South America. Most species are very free-flowering and popular with collectors. Many can be flowered easily on a sunny windowsill.

Above: The bright rose-purple flowers of Nopalxochia phyllanthoides 'German Empress' are produced very freely.

Species cultivated *N. apricus*, stem globular, depressed, shallow ribs with curved spines, not sharp, flowers large, yellow with reddish outer petals, Uruguay. *N. concinnus*, similar in shape to previous species, very free-flowering, yellow flowers with red stigma, southern Brazil. *N. floricomus*, stem globular when young becoming columnar, flowers freely produced, satin-like, yellow, Uruguay. *N. graessneri*, a very handsome species with pale green stem and many golden spines, likes semi-shade, flowers greenish-yellow, southern Brazil. *N. haselbergii*, another fine species, dense white spines on body, flowers tomato-red, can last three weeks, southern Brazil. *N. leninghausii*, one of the tallest species, golden spines, flowers yellow, southern Brazil. *N. rutilans*, dark green body, white radial spines, darker centrally, flowers pale mauve to rosy red. *N. schumannianus*, tall-growing species, woolly at top, rather long spines, flowers yellow, northern Argentina. *N. scopa*, stem cylindrical, many radial spines, flowers bright yellow, southern Brazil.

Cultivation A suitable soil mixture consists of a regular potting compost with $\frac{1}{6}$ part added of sharp sand, grit and broken brick. Pot in March every year or two, and give the plants a sunny place in the greenhouse or window. Water as often as the soil dries out, from March to September, but keep the soil dry in winter. Maintain a minimum winter temperature of 40°F (4°C) rising in summer to 65–75°F (18–24°C). Propagation is by seed sown in pans of a good seed compost in February. Keep the seed pans shaded and moist, at a temperature of 70°F (21°C), prick out the seedlings when the cotyledon has been absorbed. Offsets which form at the base of some plants can be removed and

rooted in a mixture of sharp sand and peat.

Nyctocereus

From the Greek *nyktos*, by night, and *cereus*, referring to the fact that the flowers open by night (*Cactaceae*). A genus of 7 species of greenhouse succulent perennials, natives of Mexico and Central America. The plants are at first erect but become trailing and can be used as climbers near the roof of the greenhouse. The stems are thin and with shallow ribs; they bear thin spines at the areoles and the flowers open at night.

Species cultivated *N. guatemalensis*, stems erect until old, flowers 8 inches long with pale red or reddish-yellow outer petals, white inside, Guatemala. *N. hirschtianus*, slender stems, yellow spines, flowers pale carmine to pale rose, Nicaragua. *N. serpentinus*, a favourite

Left: Notocactus tabulare is one of a number of species with attractive flowers, occasionally found in cultivation.
Below left: Notocactus apricus has a globular spiny stem and produces large yellow flowers with reddish outer petals.
Below right: Notocactus leninghausii, from Brazil, has golden spines on its rounded stems, and grows taller than any other species.

plant with collectors, stems grow very long and climbing, flowers white to rose colour, freely produced, Mexico.

Cultivation A suitable soil consists of an average compost, with $\frac{1}{6}$ part added of sharp sand, grit and broken brick. Pot in March in well-drained pots. The growth can be trained up a trellis or under the roof of the greenhouse. Water well from April to September, then reduce to none at all from November to March. In winter maintain a minimum temperature of 40°F (4°C), rising in the growing season to normal summer greenhouse temperatures. Plants can be raised from seed as for other cacti, but as it is so easy to take cuttings of small sideshoots it is not worth the trouble of raising the plants from seed. Cuttings soon root in sharp sand if the cut surfaces are first dried for a week.

Opuntia

From the Greek *Opuntus*, a town in Greece where cactus-like plants are said to have grown (*Cactaceae*). Prickly pear. A genus of greenhouse succulent plants which can also be grown in a sunny window. This is a very large genus of between 250 and 300 species, natives of the Americas and the Galapagos Islands. The plants vary in shape from having small cylindrical joints to large flat pads or tree-like growths. Some retain a small cylindrical leaf at the areole for some time. The flowers are mostly spreading and colourful, the fruits are quite often edible. For a cactus, they have large seeds. The areoles carry glochids—small tufts of short spines— and as they are barbed they are easily picked up on the fingers.

Greenhouse species cultivated *O. brasiliensis*, tree-like stem with pale green flat joints, flowers pale yellow, widely distributed in Brazil and Bolivia. *O. cylindrica*, stems tall and round with few white spines, flowers red, Ecuador, Peru. *O. dillenii*, makes a large bush, yellow glochids, large yellow flowers, West Indies, Mexico. *O. elongata*, tree-like in growth, stems oval-long, few spines, flowers wide, pale yellow, Mexico. *O. ficus-indica*, 15 feet, canary yellow flowers, bears fruits which are edible and much appreciated in America, but they have fine glochids on them which must be removed before eating, large oval pads are formed with few spines, tropical America. *O. herrfeldtii*, an erect bushy plant with a short stem, handsome species, reddish-brown glochids, flowers sulphur yellow, Mexico. *O. grandiflora*. few spines, large flowers 4 inches across, yellow with a red centre, eastern Texas. *O. macracantha*, cylindrical stem with long spines, flower orange-yellow, Cuba. *O. microdasys*, a much branched bush, very popular for window cultivation or bowl gardens, almost round pads well covered with glochids, no long spines, flowers pale yellow with reddish tips to petals, northern Mexico; there are

Right: The Prickly Pear, or Opuntia, holds its fruits around the edges of its enormous flat joints.
Below left: The flowers of Opuntia speggazzinii are a silvery-white in colour and of a thin texture and grow in groups.
Below right: Opuntia bergeriana has deep red flowers and is the plant that commonly forms thickets on the Riviera.

several varieties of this species varying according to the colour of the glochids, a white one known as *alba*, red known as *rufida*, and a pale yellow known as *pallida*. All sensitive to low winter temperatures. *O. sulphurea*, joints oval or elliptical, glochids yellowish-red, a very popular species, Argentina.

Hardy *O. engelmannii*, spreading bush, joints oval or round, flower yellow, 4 inches across, central America. *O. polyacantha*, one of the hardiest opuntias, the pads are broadly oval and

sprawl over the ground, it has many areoles close together, and whitish spines, flowers pale yellow; there are several varieties with differing coloured spines, British Columbia and Arizona. *O. vulgaris* csyn. *O. opuntia*), thick joints growing prostrate, flowers pale yellow, North America.

Greenhouse species cultivation A compost mixture consisting of an average potting compost with $\frac{1}{6}$ part added of sharp sand, grit and broken brick is suitable. Pot them in spring in a well-drained pot, just large enough to take the roots and give them a sunny position in the greenhouse or a sunny window sill. Water them from March to September, fairly freely when new growth is seen, but do not give so much that the soil remains very wet for long periods. From October to March they should not be watered at all, unless they are being grown in a heated room, when they can be watered once a month. A temperature of not less than 45°F (7°C) is required in winter, rising to 65–80°F (18–27°C) in summer.

Hardy species cultivation These must have a well-drained soil as the plants will not stand a permanently wet position. Although some opuntias will stand the winter out of doors in mild areas it must be realized that a severe winter could kill them. A sheltered spot must be found and some shelter from too much rain will help them to survive. Propagate all kinds of seed sown in a good seed compost. Cover the seeds as they are usually large, and then keep them damp, shaded and at a temperature of 70°F (21°C). Do not discard the seed pan if no seedlings appear for some time, as the seeds can still germinate after a year. Propagation may also be effected by cuttings which can be taken off at pads or joints, the base dried in the sun and set in sharp sand. Spray them occasionally and keep them in a sunny position.

Oreocereus

From the Greek *oros*, mountain and *Cereus*, i.e. *cerei* from the mountains (*Cactaceae*). A small genus of greenhouse succulent plants, sometimes

Left: Opuntia paraguensis has deep golden cup-shaped flowers. It is a plant from the warmer regions of South America.
Below left: A cluster of buds of the red flowers of Opuntia bergeriana the Prickly Pear plant, commonly seen in Mediterranean regions.
Below right: Opuntia microdasys, a plant suited to window cultivation.

placed in the genus *Borzicactus*. They are very attractive cacti which can grow up to 3 feet tall in a greenhouse, and are useful for breaking the flatness of the collection. They sometimes branch at the base and they have many white hairs with coloured spines between.

Species cultivated *O. celsianus*, stem upright up to 3 feet high, with bunches of yellow-gold spines and long white hairs, flowers small, tube-shaped, brownish-red, Peru and Bolivia. *O. hendriksenianus*, very attractive with long silky golden hairs, flowers as for *O. celsianus*, Bolivia, Peru. *O. trollii*, not as tall as previous species, very densely clothed with hairs and wood, flowers small, red, Bolivia, in the Andean Cordillera. One species, once known as *O. doelzianus*, is now classed under the genus *Morawetzia*.

Cultivation Use a potting compost with few added nutrients with $\frac{1}{6}$ part added of sharp sand, limestone chippings and broken brick. Repot every two or three years, or when the plants get too tall for the size of pot. Water from April to September, but keep the plants dry for the rest of the year. In winter maintain a minimum temperature of 40°F (4°C), rising in summer to 65–85°F (18–29°C). Propagation is by seed sown in regular seed compost, just covering the seed. Keep the pans moist, shaded and at a temperature of 70°F (21°C). Seedlings soon make sizeable plants. Or plants may be increased by cuttings of side shoots; dry the cut surfaces in the sun and root the cuttings in sharp sand and peat in equal parts.

Pachycereus

From the Greek *pachys*, thick, and the Latin *cereus*, wax-like, in reference to the stems (*Cactaceae*). A genus of 5 species of greenhouse succulent plants, rather large and branching and usually having a definite trunk. The branches are very thick and cylindrical with many definite ribs. The flowers open mainly during the day, and the plants are mostly natives of Central America. It is said that the natives use *P. pecten-aboriginum* as a comb, which accounts for its name.

Species cultivated *P. orcutii*, stems up to 10 feet, glossy green, flowers brownish, lower California. *P. pecten-aboriginum*, dark green stems up to 25 feet high, the inner petals of the flowers are white, Mexico. *P. pringlei*, dark, blue-green stems up to 40 feet high, flowers reddish on the outside and white inside, up to 2 or 3 inches long, lower California.

Cultivation The soil mixture for these plants should consist of a rich potting compost to which has been added $\frac{1}{6}$ part of coarse sand, grit or broken brick. A sunny position in the greenhouse is required. Water from March to September, but keep the compost dry and maintain a minimum temperature of 45°F (7°C) for the remainder of the year.

Top: A young plant of Oreocereus maximus, a greenhouse succulent, from South America, which can reach enormous proportions with age.
Above: A single flower of Pachycereus pecten-aboriginum. It is a greenhouse succulent reaching 7.5m (25 feet) in nature, with very colourful flowers.

Propagation is by seed sown in a good seed compost and kept moist and shaded at a temperature of 70°F (21°C) until germination takes place. Transplant the seedlings when they are large enough to handle. Cuttings taken from plants can be rooted in a mixture of coarse sand and peat, allowing the cut surface to callus over before putting the cutting in the rooting medium.

Parodia

Commemorating Dr L. R. Parodi, of Buenos Aires *(Cactaceae)*. These are greenhouse succulent perennials, small round plants with a flattened top, very free-flowering and a great favourite with collectors. There are 35 species, natives of tropical and sub-tropical South America.

Species cultivated *P. aureispina*, many short spines, mostly golden in colour, with golden-yellow flowers at the top, Argentina. *P. catamarcensis*, woolly areoles, and whitish-yellow flowers, northern Argentina. *P. chrysacanthion*, pale green globular flattened stem, with many long thin golden-yellow spines, small bright yellow flowers, Argentina. *P. mutabilis*, very shallow ribs, woolly areoles and hooked spines, golden-yellow flowers, Argentina. *P. sanguiniflora*, many bristle-like spines, hooked central spine, blood-red flowers which are very attractive, Argentina.

Cultivation Use a regular potting compost, with $\frac{1}{6}$ part added of sharp sand, grit and broken brick. The plants should be potted in March in small pots, and between March and September watered when the soil has dried out. During the resting period they should be kept quite dry. Provide a temperature of 65–75°F (18–24°C) in summer; not less than 40°F (4°C) in winter. A sunny position in the greenhouse or a very sunny window are the best places to keep them. These plants rarely, if ever, make offsets for cuttings so propagate from seed, sowing it in pans of lightly sifted seed compost, as it is very small. Do not cover it, and keep it moist, shaded and in a temperature of 70°F (21°C). The seedlings may not be large enough to prick out for a year.

Pereskia

Commemorating Nicholas F. Peiresc (1580–1627), a French patron of botany *(Cactaceae)*. Greenhouse succulent perennials, numbering about 20 species, the thin stems of which are clothed with leaves that are almost permanent. The areoles are large, with few spines; the plants are natives of tropical America. They are generally regarded as being the most primitive of the *Cactaceae*.

Species cultivated *P. aculeata*, climbing, long pointed leaves, whitish, scented flowers in clusters, Mexico, West Indies. *P. bleo*, tall, erect shrub, long thin leaves, pink flowers in clusters, Colombia, Panama. *P. conzattii*, erect branching stem, almost round leaves, pink flowers, Mexico. *P. grandiflora*, shrub with spiny stems, broad, fleshy leaves, pink flowers in clusters, very handsome, Brazil, *P. saccharosa*, tall shrub, dark green leaves, pink flowers, Paraguay.

Cultivation A good soil mixture is an average potting compost with $\frac{1}{6}$ part added of sand, grit and broken brick. Repot in March every two years. Between March and September they should be watered when the soil is almost dry, but from October–March, they need not be watered at all. Give them a minimum winter temperature of 45°F (7°C) and a summer temperature of between 65°F (18°C) and 75°F (24°C). Propagate by seed sown in a reliable seed compost in March, kept moist, shaded and at a temperature of 75°F (24°C). They may

also be propagated by cuttings taken in summer. The bases should be allowed to dry and then the cuttings should be rooted in coarse sand. These cuttings are very good for use as stocks upon which to graft epiphytic cacti such as schlumbergeras and zygocactus.

Porfiria

Commemorating Porfirio Diaz, a former Mexican president *(Cactaceae.)* These are greenhouse succulents rather similar in appearance to *Mammillaria* and by some authorities included in that genus. The habit of growth is non-grouping, there is a thick tap-root, and a round stem, flat at the top; there are no grooves on the tubercles and the flowers are produced from the upper axils. There is one species only cultivated, *P. schwartzii*, which has a round, fleshy body and small tubercles pointing outwards and upward. The areoles are woolly at first and the flowers pale pink with a lighter coloured centre; they last for several days. There is a variety. *albiflora*, with white flowers; both are natives of Mexico.

Cultivation A compost with few added nutrients is suitable, with ⅙ part of extra sand, grit and broken brick. Pot the plants in March and water them between

Above: Parodia catamarcensis, a cactus from Argentina, is in full flower here.

April and September, but only when the soil dries out. After September until March, do not water at all. In winter the temperature should be not less than 40°F (4°C), and during the growing period 65–75°F (18–24°C). These plants prefer a sunny position in the greenhouse. Propagation is by seed as for mammillarias; porfirias rarely make offsets.

Rebutia

Commemorating P. Rebut, a French cactus nurseryman *(Cactaceae)*. Greenhouse succulent perennials, very suitable for window cultivation, mostly from Argentina. In general, the species remain very dwarf and can be grown in pots no larger than 3 inches. They flower very freely.

Species cultivated *R. albiflora*, fine snowy white spines, flowers white; it requires a little more heat in winter than most other species. *R. chrysacantha*, round, flat-topped stem, golden-yellow bristle-like spines, flowers pink. *R. deminuta*, round stem, flowers red or orange round the base of the stem. *R. fiebrigii* (syn. *Aylostera fiebrigii*), round

spiny stem, red flowers from higher up the plant than on most species, Bolivia. *R. minuscula*, round stem flat at the top, many red flowers at the base, very popular and easily grown plant suitable for windows or bowl gardens. *R. senilis*, round stem, white spines, flowers carmine-red; attractive species, *R. violaciflora*, round stem, flowers deep lilac-rose appearing from the sides.

Cultivation Give the rebutias a potting compost with few added nutrients mixed with ⅙ part added of sharp sand, grit and broken brick. They should be repotted in March every year in small pots. Keep them dry in winter but water from March to September while growing. The temperature from March to October should be 65–75°F (18–24°C), and 45°F (7°C) in winter. Propagation is by seed sown in a good seed compost in March; keep it moist but not wet, shaded and at a temperature of 75°F (24°C). This is an easy method of increase. It is also possible to propagate by detaching and rooting offsets, but as these are firmly joined to the parent plant, it is probable that a bad scar will be left.

Rhipsalidopsis

From the Greek *rhips*, a willow or wicker work, and *opsis*, like, in reference to the similarity to the genus *Rhipsalis*, which has pliable interwoven branches *(Cactaceae)*. A genus of two species, greenhouse succulent many-branched, shrub-like perennials. The stems may be erect or hanging, and the plants resemble a miniature *Zygocactus*. The flowers appear at the areoles on the end of a joint. The only species cultivated is *R. rosea*, from the forests of Brazil, which has rosy-pink flowers with a short tube.

Cultivation The plants should be grown in a rich porous soil; an average potting compost will be suitable with extra leafmould and a little extra sand to increase porosity. They do not need a very hot position in the greenhouse and should be shaded from June to September. Water freely from March to September, but keep the soil dry in winter, when the plant needs a minimum temperature of 45°F (7°C). Propagation is usually by means of cuttings taken at the joints on the parent plant, which are dried for a few days and placed on sharp sand. If these are sprayed occasionally, roots will soon form. Pieces of the stem may also be grafted on to epiphyllum or pereskia stock, but rhipsalidopsis will grow well on its own roots.

Rhipsalis

From the Greek *rhips*, a willow or wicker work, in reference to the slender interlacing branches *(Cactaceae)*. A genus of about 60 species, greenhouse succulent perennials, mainly epiphytic and growing in nature in forests where there is considerable humidity and plenty of moisture. They are found in tropical America, the West Indies, East and West Africa and Sri Lanka. Many grow in the forks of trees where there may be plenty of decaying leaves and bird manure.

Species cultivated *R. cassutha*, a hanging bush, flowers small greenish-white or cream, Brazil and tropical Africa. *R. cèreuscula*, mistletoe cactus, well-branched stems, flowers white with a yellow stripe, small white berries, Brazil. *R. crispata*, wide flat stems with wavy margins, flowers pale yellow, Brazil. *R. grandiflora*, cylindrical stems, flowers small, greenish-white, Brazil. *R. houlletiana*, pale green flat stems, toothed along the margins, flowers cream, Brazil. *R. paradoxa*, stems triangular in cross-section, each joint twisted in relation to the next so that an angle is above and below a flat side, flowers white, Brazil.

Cultivation These plants require a compost richer than that needed by most cacti, consisting of 4 parts of loam, 2 parts of peat and 2 parts of sharp sand. To 1 bushel of this mixture add 1 ounce of ground chalk and 8 ounces of a good base fertilizer. The plants must not have too sunny a position in the greenhouse, and the soil should not be kept dry in warm weather. Water freely from March to September but once a month only between September and March. The temperature in winter should be not less than 45°F (7°C), and in summer the plants can be put out of doors in partial shade. Propagation is by seed sown in John Innes seed compost in pans at a temperature of 70°F (21°C), or by stem cuttings rooted in sharp sand and peat.

Schlumbergera

Commemorating F. Schlumberger, owner of a famous plant collection (*Cactaceae*). A genus of a few species of succulent perennials, suitable for the greenhouse or sunny window. The plants are rather similar in form to *Zygocactus*, but the stems are a darker green and stouter, with pronounced notches on the sides of

Left: Rebutia minuscula, a popular and easily-grown plant for window-sills which produces numerous red flowers at the base of the rounded stems.
Below left: The orange-carmine flowers of Rebutia krainziana form a ruff around the base of the stem.
Below right: Rebutia senilis kesselringiana.

Top left: Rhipsalidopsis rosea 'Electra' has pendent pink flowers, produced from the areoles at the ends of the joints.
Top right: The small flowers of the Rhipsalis warmingiana are white and appear along the margins of the leaves.
Left: Rhipsalis prismatica, an epiphytic plant, has slender, much-branched stems.
Above: The Easter Cactus, Schlumbergera gaertneri, flowers very freely in April and May.

the stems. The flowers appear in spring from areoles at the tips of the joints, and are very freely produced.

Species cultivated *S. gaertneri*, Easter cactus, very free-flowering even on small plants, flat, deeply notched stems, flowers bright scarlet, April-May, Brazil. *S. russelliana*, violet-pink, spring, Brazil.

Cultivation An average potting compost is suitable, with added roughage if the soil is not porous enough. Repot after flowering each year, and keep shaded in summer whether in a greenhouse or out of doors. Water freely from the beginning of March to September, otherwise once a fortnight will be sufficient. The winter temperature should be not less than 50°F (10°C), rising to about 65°F (18°C) between March and September. Plants are easily propagated from cuttings of short pieces of stem, rooted in equal parts of coarse sand and peat. Spray the cuttings every other day or so and pot them up when the roots have formed. They may also be propagated by grafting on to *Pereskia*, or any other upright stock, to form an 'umbrella' type of plant.

Selenicereus

From the Greek *selene*, moon, and *cereus*, a reference to the flowers opening at night *(Cactaceae)*. A genus of 25 or so species of greenhouse succulent plants with slender, trailing stems, which can be trained as climbers in the greenhouse. They often have long aerial roots.

Species cultivated *S. brevispinus*, long, ribbed stems with short spines, flowers with greenish-brown sepals, white petals, Mexico. *S. grandiflorus*, queen of the night, long stems 1 inch thick, large spectacular flower bud, brownish-green sepals, white petals, heavy scent of vanilla, open soon after sunset and fade in the morning. Jamaica. *S. grusonianus*, very long, dark green stems, very free flowering, flowers white, not scented. *S. macdonaldiae*, fast growing, good for training under the roof of the greenhouse, free flowering, flowers large white, with reddish-purple sepals, early summer, Uruguay and Argentina. *S. pteranthus*, king of the night, purple-green stems, flowers large, white or cream, purple-yellow sepals, June, July, Central-America.

Cultivation Use a compost with few added nutrients with $\frac{1}{6}$ part added of sharp sand, grit and broken brick. The plants should be repotted when pot bound, or every two or three years, and put in a sunny position in the greenhouse, or bedded out in the greenhouse border. During the winter the temperature should not fall · below 40–45°F (4–7°C); in summer ordinary greenhouse warmth is satisfactory. From October to March, the soil should be kept dry, and from March to September the plants should be watered when the soil dries out. Propagate by seed sown

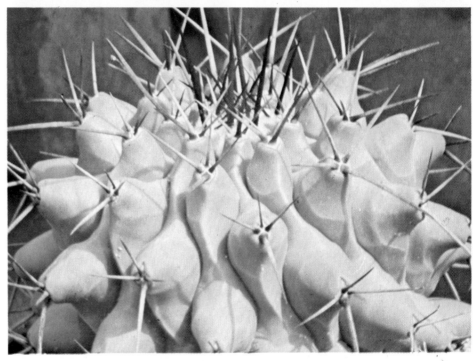

Top left: Selinicereus grandiflorus, Queen of the Night, has a spectacular flower which is strongly vanilla scented and open during one night only.
Top right: Selenicereus coniflorus, a trailing succulent which blooms at night.
Above: Thelocactus lophothele a globular cactus, has long spines.

in well-drained pots as for other cacti or by cuttings of young stems. Dry the cut end and root in sharp sand. Spray the cuttings occasionally while the roots are forming.

Thelocactus

From the Greek *thele*, a nipple, and cactus, referring to the tuberculate ribs (*Cactaceae*). A genus of 17 species of greenhouse succulent perennials from Mexico and the southern United States, mostly round plants with shallow ribs, divided into wart-like protuberances. The flowers are quite large and open during the day.

Species cultivated *T. bicolor*, flowers large, violet-red, borne near the top of the plant, Texas and Mexico. *T. hexaedrophurus*, stem very woolly at top, flowers pinkish-white. *T. lophothele*, grey-green body, flowers pale yellow with red stripes. *T. pottsii*, round and flat-topped, flowers purple. *T. rinconadensi*, young areoles have whitish wool, flowers white. *T. sausseri*, strong central spines, flowers purple-red, an attractive species.

Cultivation A good compost with few added nutrients mixed with $\frac{1}{6}$ part added of sand, grit and broken brick. The plants should be repotted every two years in March in pots just large enough to take them. Give them a sunny shelf in the greenhouse and water between March and September when the soil dries out, but keep the soil dry from October to March. The minimum winter temperature should be 40°F (4°C), and in summer the normal greenhouse temperature is suitable. Propagation is by seed sown in a good seed compost kept moist and shaded at 70°F (21°C). Plants rarely make branches or offsets and so seed raising is necessary to increase stock.

Trichocereus

From the Greek *thrix*, *trichos*, a hair, and *cereus*, in reference to the hairs produced at the areoles from which the flowers appear *(Cactaceae)*. A genus of 40 species of greenhouse succulent perennials from South America with erect columnar stems, sometimes branching at the base. They are mostly well clothed with spines, and have many ribs. The flowers are usually nocturnal, appearing at an areole through a thick tuft of wool.

Species cultivated *T. bridgesii*, freely branching, flowers white, nocturnal but lasting during the following morning; often used for hedging in its native Bolivia; a monstrous form is often grown. *T. candicans*, thick stem, branches freely from the base, flowers large, white, sweetly scented, north-western Argentina. *T. pachanoi*, can grow to 18 feet freely branching, the best stock on which to graft other cacti, stems, blue-green, flowers very large, white, southern Ecuador. *T. pasacana*, up to 15 feet, stems 1½ feet thick, strongly spined, flowers white, fruits edible, north-western Argentina and Bolivia. *T. peruvianus*, to 12 feet, freely branching, young stems bluish-green, flowers long, white, scented, Peru. *T. schickendantzii*, stems short, thick, making compact groups, flowers large, white, sweetly scented, north-western Argentina. *T. spachianus*, spines golden-yellow to brown, flowers nocturnal, green outside and white inside, much used for grafting as strong stems are quickly formed from rooted off-shoots.

Cultivation These plants do best in a compost with few added nutrients with ⅙ part added of sharp sand, grit and broken brick. They should be repotted in spring every three years or when they become too large for the pot. Keep the soil dry from October to March, but water when it dries out between March and September. The minimum winter temperature should be 40°F (4°C); during the growing period the plants can be given full sunshine and normal greenhouse temperatures. Propagation is by seed sown in reliable seed compost uncovered, and kept shaded and moist at a temperature of 70°F (21°C). Species which produce offshoots may be propagated by cuttings, dried for a week and then inserted shallowly in sharp sand.

Zygocactus

From the Greek *zygon*, a yoke, and *Cactus*, possibly referring to the shape of the stem joints *(Cactaceae)*. Christmas cactus. A genus of a single species, an epiphytic greenhouse cactus, placed by some botanists as a hybrid in the genus *Schlumbergera*. The species is *Z. truncatus*, from eastern Brazil. It has flat, short stems with small areoles, minute spines and claw-like joints. Cerise-red flowers are freely-produced from the ends of the joints from December to

February; vars. *altensteinii*, teeth on stems more pronounced, flowers brick-red; *crenatus*, flowers small, bluish-violet; *delicatus*, growth more erect, flowers pale pink.

Cultivation *Z. truncatus* is easy to grow, either on its own roots or grafted on to a tall stock to make an umbrella-shaped specimen. Use an average potting compost with added leafmould. Repot every two years or when the plant becomes too large for its pot, repotting when flowering has ceased. In winter maintain a minimum temperature of 50°F (10°C), increasing this to 60°F (16°C) as buds form. Water when the soil has almost dried out, throughout the winter. In June plants may be placed out of doors in semi-shade. Plants do not like a sunny position in an un-

Top: Trichocereus spachianus is covered with golden-yellow to brown spines, The flowers open at night. Above: Zygocactus truncatus, the Christmas Cactus, is easy to grow and produces cerise-red flowers in winter.

shaded greenhouse; they do better in a medium-lighted room in the house. Give them a weak liquid feed after flowering. When plants are in bud do not move them and at this time, in particular, protect them from draughts. The causes of bud drop are too wet or too dry a soil or a changeable atmosphere. Propagation is by cuttings which are best taken in early summer and rooted in sharp sand, spraying them occasionally. Or plants may be grafted on to *Pereskia* stock.

Successful succulents

The Crassulaceae

Adromischus

From the Greek *akros*, strong, and *miskos*, flower stem *(Crassulaceae)*. Dwarf-growing succulents, herb-like, mostly making clumps. Fleshy leaves, round, flat or cylindrical, mottled with reddish-brown.

Species cultivated *A. alstonii*, leaves narrow and flattened, dull red, to 3 inches, S.W. Africa. *A. clavifolius*, leaves club-shaped, 2 inches, smooth, green, sometimes reddish; small greenish-pink flowers, Cape Province. *A. hemisphaericus*, grows to 12 inches high, leaves compressed light green with thin waxy layer, sometimes reddish without blotches, flowers on long stalk, small whitish-red, South-west Africa. *A. maculatus*, (sometimes found under *Cotyledon maculatus*), leaves round to oval, green, flecked with reddish-brown on both sides, flowers small on spikes, reddish-white, Cape Province. *A. rotundifolius*, leaves roundish-oval, green with waxy dots, flowers numerous on stalk, bright pink, Cape Province. *A. triebneri*, dwarf shrub, leaves wedge shaped, narrow at base, green-red, flower spike long with many small reddish-green flowers, Cape Province.

Cultivation These succulents require a very porous soil and should be grown in a greenhouse or on a sunny window sill in a temperature not below 45°F (7°C). Propagation is from leaf-cuttings or by seed.

Aeonium

An ancient name for *A. arboreum* or a similar plant *(Crassulaceae)*. Succulent plants for greenhouse or for summer bedding, especially edging, from the Canary Islands and the Mediterranean region.

Species cultivated *A. arboreum*, stems up to 4 feet high, leaves in form of rosette, flat at top, flowers in long racemes, golden-yellow; var. *foliis purpureis* has dark purple leaves. *A. ciliatum*, many stemmed leaves rounded, pointed at tip, flowers whitish-green. *A. nobile*, short stemmed with large leaves, rosettes very large and fleshy, light olive-green sometimes sticky, flowers coppery-scarlet, flowers after about seven years and then dies. Plants need plenty of warmth, sun and moisture; raise from seed. *A. tabulaeforme*, low growth with large rosettes like plates, up to 1 foot across, leaves large, wavy, green turning reddish when

old. Flowers sulphur-yellow; plant dies after flowering.

Cultivation Provide a porous potting compost with few added nutrients, plus $\frac{1}{6}$ part of coarse, sharp sand. Broken brick and granulated charcoal may be added to extra sand if not sharp enough. Position, greenhouse or sunny window. For bedding soil must be well drained. Pot March to April. Water when soil is dry. March to October, give none in

Below: Adromischus cooperii, a South African succulent, has wedge-shaped leaves.
Bottom: The rosette leaves of Aeonium arboreum foliis purpureis.

winter. Temperature in summer 55–75°F (13–24°C), minimum in winter 45°F (7°C). Propagation is by seed sown in a good seed compost, in early spring. Do not cover seeds; temperature 65–70°F (18–21°C); or by stem cuttings or leaves inserted in sharp sand and peat in equal parts. Allow cut parts to dry first.

Bryophyllum

From the Greek *bryo*, to sprout, and *phyllon*, leaf, a reference to the fact that the leaves bear plantlets round their edges *(Crassulaceae)*. Greenhouse succulent plants which grow tall and the leaves produce small plantlets at the notches. They are easy to grow and flower even on a window sill. One plant can drop hundreds of small plantlets in a season. The flowers are produced in late autumn or early winter in large umbels, long lasting. Bryophyllums are occasionally found under *Kalanchoe*.

Species cultivated *B. daigremontianum*, a well-known species with well-notched leaves, pale green with red markings, plantlets produced in profusion on the leaves, flowers grey-green, plants can be placed out of doors in summer. *B. tubiflora*, tall stems with many narrow tubular leaves, like small caterpillars, plantlets on ends, flowers red to violet. Both species are from Madagascar.

Cultivation The compost should be a porous soil, with few added nutrients and mixed with a sixth part of sharp sand or broken brick. Pot in March or April, water freely during warm weather, and very little in late autumn and winter. Prune the old flowering stem back to top leaves, temperature 65–75°F (18–24°C), in summer, 45°F (7°C), in winter, when kept dry. Propagation is by seeds sown on the surface of a fine tilth of a good seed compost, in a temperature of 70°F (21°C); do not cover seed. Shade seedlings from sun when small. The small plantlets which appear on the leaves will often form roots while still on the plant. They are easily detached to make fresh plants, the simplest form of propagation.

Cotyledon

From the Greek *kotyle*, a cup, referring to the cup-like leaves of one species *(Crassulaceae)*. Evergreen succulents; a large genus of shrubs or semi-shrubs, usually forming clumps, leaves mostly fleshy, flower cluster tall, branched, flowers mostly pendent.

Species cultivated *C. decussata*, 2–3 feet,

leaves green with red tips, flowers yellow with red stripes, Cape Province. *C. grandiflora*, dwarf growing, flowers orange-red, Table Mountain. *C. macracantha*, 1–2 feet, flowers red, Cape Province. *C. orbiculata*, small shrub, thick roundish leaves with point at tip, white-grey with red edges, flowers yellowish-red, South-West Africa. *C. paniculata*, shrub with very thick, fleshy stem, flowers reddish yellow-green, Cape Province. *C. undulata*, erect shrub up to 2½ feet tall, leaves broad with wavy margins, whitish in colour, flowers on long stalk, orange-yellow, Cape Province.

Cultivation Pot in March in a regular potting compost, plus a sixth part of roughage in the form of grit, coarse sand and broken brick. Keep in sunny position in the house or greenhouse. Plants may be bedded out for summer but cannot stand frost. Water as often as the soil dries out from March to September. Temperatures: 65°F (18°C) in growing period, 40°F (4°C) in winter. Plants are easily raised from seed sown on top of a good seed compost and not covered, in a temperature of 70°F (21°C), or by cuttings taken in summer, the cut surface allowed to dry and then rooted in sharp sand.

Crassula

From the Latin *crassus*, thick, referring to the fleshy leaves *(Crassulaceae)*. Greenhouse evergreen succulent plants, a very large genus with between 200 and 300 species. Mostly perennial herbs, many with a tuberous rootstock, varying from very dwarf types resembling bird droppings, to 3–4 foot tall shrubs. Many species are suitable for room culture and varied types are grown in collections of cacti and other succulents.

Species cultivated *C. arborescens*, shrub, 3–4 feet high, leaves fleshy, grey-green edged with red, flowers white to pink but rarely produced, Cape Province. *C. columella*, small shrub, stems closely packed with short leaves, which are brownish green with minute hairs, flowers greenish-white, Cape Province. *C. corallina*, very dwarf, short thick leaves tightly packed round stems, flowers white, South-West Africa. *C. deceptrix*, low-growing herb, whitish-grey leaves, flowers white, growing period in winter, Namaqualand. *C. falcata* (syn. *Rochea falcata*), erect fleshy stems with thick leaves, flattened and pointed at the tip, flowers scarlet to orange-red, a beautiful plant for green-

Top: Bryophyllum tubiflorum attracts attention because of the way that tiny plantlets form on the ends of the leaves. These eventually drop off and are easily rooted to form a ready means of increase.
Right: Crassula columnaris dies down after flowering and does not make offsets.

house or window culture, Cape Province. *C. justi-corderoyi*, forming clumps, leaves small, dark green with red spots, flowers reddish, suitable for bowl gardens, South-West Africa. *C. lycopodioides*, slender stems, erect to prostrate, closely covered with small leaves, flowers tiny, yellowish-white, offensive smelling, popular plant for window culture, South-West Africa. *C. rupestris* (syn. *C. perfossa*), dwarf shrub with prostrate stems, grey-green leaves with brown dots, small yellowish flowers, Cape Province.

Cultivation Provide a compost consisting of an average potting compost plus a sixth part of sharp sand, grit and broken brick. Pot in March and place in a sunny position on a shelf in the greenhouse. Water gradually in March, increase during summer and decrease in September, keep dry for winter. Temperature March–September 65–70°F (18–21°C), winter not below 45°F (7°C). Some of the dwarf, mimicry types require very careful treatment and must not be overwatered at any time, especially those which develop a small corm or caudex. Propagation is by seed sown on a good seed compost in pans. Keep the compost moist at a temperature of 70°F (21°C), shade the seedlings from sunshine; they are liable to damp off if kept too wet. Alternatively cuttings may be taken in summer, the cut part allowed to dry, then rooted in sharp sand and peat in equal parts; spray at times but do not keep the cuttings too wet while the roots are forming.

Echeveria
Commemorating Atanasio Echeverria, Mexican botanical artist *(Crassulaceae)*. Greenhouse and half-hardy, low-growing succulent plants, formerly included in *Cotyledon;* mostly of upright growth with large fleshy leaves in rosettes, many well coloured and waxy in appearance.

Species cultivated *E. agavoides*, very thick fleshy leaves, long and pointed, flowers red and carmine, central Mexico. *E. bella*, forms clumps, flowers orange-yellow, Mexico. *E. gibbiflora*, stems strong, erect, leaves broad and shiny, flowers light red with yellow centre, Mexico; vars. *caruncula*, with raised rough parts to the centre of leaf; *metallica*, leaves bronze edged with red. *E. harmsii* (syns. *E. elegans*, *Oliveranthus elegans*), much branched shrubby plant, 1–1½ feet tall, each branch ending in a rosette of leaves, large flowers, 1 inch long, red, tipped yellow, a most handsome species, Mexico.

Cultivation The soil mixture should be made from an average potting compost with a sixth part added of grit, sand and broken brick. Pot the plants in March and place them in a sunny position. Old plants get very leggy and lose their lower leaves. The tops can then be cut off and rooted and the old stem

Above: Echeveria elegans makes an attractive pot plant for the home. Left: Echeveria gibbiflora, an attractive succulent plant.

will send out fresh shoots. Water from April to September, but give none in winter unless the plants are in a warm room when they should be watered once a month. They may be planted out of doors in early June and removed to the greenhouse in September. Some, particularly *E. gibbiflora metallica*, are used in summer bedding schemes as edging plants. Propagation is by seed sown in a good seed compost at a temperature of 70°F (21°C), in early spring. Shade the seedlings from strong sunshine, prick them out when large enough. Plants are also readily increased from cuttings, including leaves. It is also possible to flower young shoots. Flower scapes cut off and dried can make roots.

Graptopetalum
From the Greek *grapho*, to write, *petalon*, petal, referring to the markings on the petals of some species *(Crassulaceae)*.

Greenhouse succulent plants which are sometimes stemless or have many branched thick succulent stems. The thick leaves are in the form of a rosette and have a waxy coating. Flowers are borne on an axillary stem, the petals being joined for half their length then spreading wide. These plants are closely related to *Echeveria* and *Pachyphytum*.

Species cultivated As well as true species there are also many intergeneric hybrids in cultivation, which masquerade under true species names. *G. amethystinum*, long stems, thick ovate leaves bluish-grey, flowers yellowish-green, Mexico. *G. filiferum*, stemless forming large mats, leaves about three times as long as broad, light green with a brown bristle at the end, flowers white spotted red, Mexico. *G. pachyphyllum*, short thick leaves green-grey, flowers white. *G. paraguayense* (syn. *G. weinbergii*) long stems, thick obovate grey leaves ending in a point, flowers white.

Cultivation The compost should consist of an average compost with a sixth part added of coarse sand, grit or broken brick. Repot each year in March. Place plants in full sun in an airy part of the greenhouse. Water from March to October. Plants benefit from being placed in the open garden, giving protection from rain, from March to September. Beware of frosts. Maintain a minimum winter temperature of 45°F (7°C). Propagation is by seed sown in a good seed compost. Lightly cover the seeds with sifted compost, keep moist and shaded at 70°F (21°C) until seedlings appear, then give more light. Propagation can also be done by taking leaf cuttings or removing off-sets and rooting

Above right: The fleshy leaves of Graptopetalum pachyphyllum.
Right: Greenovia aurea.
Below: Kalanchoe pumila.

them in equal parts of sharp sand and peat. Straggly plants should have the terminal rosette cut off and re-rooted. The basal portion of the original plant should be kept as this will throw out more off-sets.

Greenovia

Commemorating George Bellas Greenough, early nineteenth-century geologist *(Crassulaceae)*. Greenhouse succulents from the Canary Islands, similar in growth to *Aeonium*, but lacking the tall stems of the latter. The leaves are in the form of a rosette which closes up like a fir cone when subjected to intense sunshine. The rosette extends to form a flower stem, which branches freely at the end and carries many bright yellow flowers. Most rosettes die after the plant has flowered. All plants form offsets freely.

Species cultivated *G. aizoon*, leaves covered with hairs, yellow flowers; grows high above sea level. *G. aurea*, forms low cushions, flowers dark golden yellow. *G. dodrantalis*, dainty small shrub, flowers yellow.

Cultivation Greenovias do best in a very sandy compost, made up from an average potting compost, with a fifth part added of sharp sand, broken brick and granulated charcoal. Pot in spring in well-drained pots; keep the pots on a shelf in the greenhouse from autumn to spring, out of doors in a sunny position during the summer.

Water well when growing, and maintain a temperature of 40–50°F (4–10°C) in winter; usual summer temperatures. Propagation is by seeds sown as for *Aeonium*, or by cuttings which root easily either in the greenhouse or out of doors.

Kalanchoë

From the native Chinese name for one species *(Crassulaceae)*. Kalanchoës are succulent greenhouse perennials, with fragrant flowers, first introduced in the late eighteenth century. The Malagash species require a temperature of not less than 50°F (10°C) in winter, but other species will stand a winter temperature of 40°F (4°C). Many are winter to spring-flowering, and they can be placed out of doors in the summer. The bryophyllums are now considered to be a sub-genus of kalanchoë.

Species cultivated *K. beharensis*, tall, thick, hairy stem, large triangular leaves covered in dense brown felt, Malagasy. *K. blossfeldiana*, 1 foot, scarlet, winter, an excellent plant for pot work; 'Tom Thumb' and 'Vulcan' are two good miniature varieties, Malagasy. *K. campanulata*, bright red bell-like flowers on tall stem, Malagasy. *K. eriophylla*, thin, woolly stems, leaves united at base, covered in felt, Malagasy. *K. flammea*, orange-red, Somalia. *K. longiflora*, yellowish-orange, Natal. *K. marmorata*, spotted leaves, white, keep warm in winter, Eritrea. *K. pumila*, leaves covered with grey-pink wax, flowers red-violet, Malagasy. *K. rhombo-pilosa*, small shrubby plant, leaves spotted dark maroon, flowers small, Malagasy.

Cultivation A porous, nourishing soil is necessary. A potting compost with few added nutrients may be used with $\frac{1}{6}$ part of sharp sand or other similar material added. Pot in March and September. They can be put in an airy place in the greenhouse or outside in the summer. Temperature can be the normal seasonal one for out of doors, or 50–70°F (10–21°C) in the greenhouse. When the plants get leggy, cut off the tops; these can be re-rooted in sharp sand. Propagate by seed sown in a good seed compost in pans in a temperature of 70°F (21°C) in March. Do not cover the smaller seeds. Seedlings grow quickly in close warmth. Propagate also by cuttings taken from old stems, dried, and rooted in sharp sand, and by leaves laid flat on sharp sand.

Lenophyllum
Derivation uncertain, but possibly from the classical name *Lens* (from another genus with lens-shaped seeds), and the Greek *phyllon*, a leaf *(Crassulaceae)*. A small genus of low-growing greenhouse succulent plants, related to *Echeveria*, with opposite leaves, spiralling up the short stems. Yellow flowers are carried on terminal branches.
Species cultivated *L. acutifolium*, up to 4 inches, leaves long and thin, California. *L. guttatum*, leaves grey-green spotted with maroon dots, upper surface grooved, Mexico. *L. pusillum*, long narrow leaves, underside keeled, Mexico.

Cultivation The compost should consist of an average compost with a $\frac{1}{5}$ part added of coarse sand, grit, or broken brick. Repot each year in March. Water from March to September. During the growing season plants require as much sun as possible and benefit from being placed in the open garden. Minimum winter temperature 45°F (7°C). Propagation is by seed sown on a good seed compost. Lightly cover seed with sifted compost and keep moist and shaded at 70°F (21°C) until seedlings appear, then give more light. These plants are also easy to propagate by division or by taking leaf-cuttings.

Pachyphytum
From the Greek *pachys*, thick, and *phytos*, a plant, in reference to the stems and leaves which are much thickened *(Crassulaceae)*. These are succulent plants for the greenhouse, or they can be grown in a well-lit window. They are small shrubs with fleshy leaves, and the flowers are produced on a long drooping stem. There are 12 species, all natives of Mexico.
Species cultivated *P. bracteosum*, 12 inches, a thick stem with greyish-white fleshy leaves in a rosette formation, large bright red flowers. *P. compactum*, short stem with crowded cylindrical leaves and reddish-green flowers. *P. heterosepalum*, very thick leaves, green to pinkish-red flowers on a long stem. *P. hookeri*, small shrub up to 2 feet, thick fleshy leaves pointing upward and

Below: Lenophyllum guttatum, a green house succulent plant from Mexico.

light red flowers with yellow tips. *P. longifolium*, spreading habit of growth, short stem and club-shaped leaves, dark red flowers. *P. oviferum*, short stem, very thick almost round leaves with a white bloom on them, bright red flowers.

Cultivation These succulents prefer a mixture of potting compost with few added nutrients with $\frac{1}{6}$ part added of sharp sand. They prefer a semi-shaded position in the greenhouse or can be grown on a window-sill and must be repotted in spring every two years. Water during the growing season between March and September, but keep the soil fairly dry during the winter, watering once a month when no frost is likely. They may be increased from seed in the same way that echeverias are, or by cuttings of offshoots dried and rooted in sharp sand, or by leaf-cuttings laid on sharp sand and sprayed occasionally.

Rochea
Commemorating the early nineteenth-century French botanical writer, François de la Roche *(Crassulaceae)*. A genus of four species of greenhouse succulent plants from South Africa. They are semi-shrubby, with leaves occurring in pairs, and the flowers developing at the tips of the shoots. They make good house plants.
Species cultivated *R. coccinea*, 20 inches, leaves thickly produced in four ranks, up to 1 inch long, flowers bright red, produced in profusion, July. *R. odoratissima*, erect shoots, loosely leaved, flowers pink. *R. versicolor*, 2-feet thick fleshy stems, with many dark green

leaves, flowers white, pink, yellow or bright red, spring.

Cultivation The soil mixture should consist of a rich potting compost with $\frac{1}{6}$ part added of coarse sand, grit or broken brick. Frequent repotting will be necessary. In winter a minimum temperature of 45°F (7°C) should be maintained, and only sufficient water given to prevent undue shrivelling of the leaves. In summer any bright sunny position is satisfactory and water can be freely given. These plants do well planted in the open garden on a well-drained site during summer when the leaves will turn bright red. The flowers are freely carried in spring and early summer. Propagation is mainly by stem cuttings taken at any time during the growing period and rooted in a mixture of coarse sand and peat. These plants have been freely hybridised for the florist's potted-plant trade and are available in several flower colours.

Sedum

From the Latin *sedo*, to sit, in reference to the manner in which some species attach themselves to rocks and walls (*Crassulaceae*). A genus of some 600 species of annual, biennial or perennial, succulent, xerophytic plants, natives of the temperate or colder regions of the northern hemisphere, with a few natives of warmer regions such as central Africa or Peru. The plants have very fleshy leaves, and several species spread over the ground as creepers. *S. acre*, the stone crop, is one of a number of native British plants. Many species and hybrids are suitable for growing on rock gardens or dry walls; others are excellent plants for the herbaceous border.

Hardy species cultivated The following is only a selection of the many that can be grown. *S. acre*, stone crop, wallpepper, mat-forming, flowers yellow, May and June, Europe (including Britain), Asia; vars. *aureum*, leaves and stem ends bright gold in spring; *elegans*, silver. *S. aizoon*, 12 inches, yellow to orange, July, China. *S. album*, 4 inches, flowers white or red, summer, Europe (including Britain), Africa, Asia. *S. cauticola*, 4–6 inches, rose-crimson, autumn, Japan. *S. elongatum* (syn. *S. bupleuroides*), hairy leaves, flowers dark purple, May and June, Himalaya, China. *S. kamtschaticum*, 6 inches, orange-yellow, June to September, northern Asia; var. *variegatum*, leaves with cream margins, flowers bright yellow. *S. maximum*, 1–3 feet, flowers greenish-white, summer, Europe; var. *atropurpureum*, stem and leaves deep red, flowers deep pink, late summer. *S. middendorffianum*, 4–6 inches, purplish leaves, flowers yellow, July to August, Siberia. *S. oreganum*, cushion-forming to 3 inches, flowers golden, July to August, western North America. *S. roseum*, rose root, 6–12 inches, greenish or yellow, May, northern hemisphere. *S. rupestre*, mat-forming, flowers yellow,

July, Europe (including Britain). *S. spathulifolium*, 3–4 inches, yellow, May to June, North America; var. 'Cappa Blanca', leaves with white meal, flowers bright yellow. *S. spectabile*, 1–1½ feet, wide, flat-topped clusters of pink flowers, late summer, China; the cultivar 'Brilliant' has deeper coloured flowers. *S. spurium*, 6 inches, white to crimson, July to August, Persia, Caucasus; vars.

Rocheas, with their bright flowers, are grown in Britain as greenhouse succulents, sometimes as pot plants indoors.

Top: Rochea subulata with white flowers;

Above: Rochea coccinea flowers in July with bright red blooms carried at the top of a stem thickly covered in four-ranked leaves.

roseum, mat-forming, flowers deep pink; Schorbusser Blut', coppery coloured foliage, flowers deep red, late summer, autumn. *S. stribrnyi*, to 6 inches, bright yellow, July, Bulgaria, Greece. *S. tele-phium*, orpine. 1–1½ feet, red-purple, August to September, Europe (including Britain), vars. 'Autumn Joy', salmon-pink and bronze, September to October; 'Munstead Red', deep red; *variegatum*, cream variegated leaves. *S.* 'Weihenstephener Gold', mat-forming, flowers golden, summer.

Tender species cultivated *S. alamosanum*, 3–5 inches, reddish-white, March, north-western Mexico. *S. bellum*, 3–6 inches, mealy leaves, flowers white, April–May, Mexico. *S. dasyphyllum*, 1–2 inches, pink, June, Mediterranean coast. *S. hintonii*, leaves and stems covered in white hairs, flowers greenish-white, Mexico. *S. longipes*, 8 inches, purple, January, Mexico. *S. modestum*, hairy, flowers whitish-red, Morocco. *S. morganianum*, long trailing stems, flowers purple, at ends of stems, good for hanging baskets in the greenhouse, summer, Mexico. *S. pachyphyllum*, almost cylindrical leaves with red tips, flowers light yellow, April, Mexico. *S. pulvinatum*, flowers white, Mexico. *S. stahlii*, 4–8 inches, reddish leaves, flowers yellow, late summer, Mexico.

Cultivation The hardy species will grow in any porous soil, on sunny borders, or rock gardens; some will grow in wall pockets, or on the tops of walls themselves. Plant between November and April. The tender species require a potting compost with few added nutrients with ⅙ part added of sharp sand, grit and broken brick. A sunny position in the greenhouse, in pots or pans, suits them and they should be potted in spring. Keep the soil dry in winter, and in summer water as the soil dries out. The minimum temperature in winter is 40°F (4°C), and 55–65°F (13–18°C) in summer. Propagation is by cuttings or divisions of plants or, with many species, by taking leaf cuttings and placing them in sharp sand. Also by seed sown in a good seed compost, the seedlings being pricked out when they are large enough to handle.

Sempervivum

From the Latin *semper*, always, and *vivo*, 'I live', an allusion to the tenacity of life common to these plants *(Crassulaceae)*. House Leek. Hardy succulent perennials from the mountains of Europe; some species are found in Britain. There are

Top: Sedum hispanicum has pinkish-white flowers and is found in the mountainous regions from Switzerland to Persia.
Centre left: Sedum spethulifolium is a low-growing species with bright yellow flowers in June.
Centre right: Sedum spectabile.
Right: Sedum cauticola.

25 species but many varieties and hybrids, can be difficult to identify accurately. The plants consist of close rosettes of leaves, some pointed, and many with fine cobweb-like hairs which form from tip to tip of the leaves. The flowers appear in a terminal inflorescence and the rosettes from which they come die when flowering has finished, but are replaced by others.

Species cultivated *S. arachnoideum*, cobweb house leek, groups of small rosettes of leaves joined together at the tips with fine white hairs, flowers pinkish-carmine, July, Pyrenees, Alps. *S. arenarium*, leaves light green, flushed red, tall flower stem, flowers pale yellow, August, Tyrol. *S. ciliosum*, large hairy rosettes, leaves grey-green, flowers greenish-yellow, July, Bulgaria, *S. grandiflorum*, very large rosettes, flowers greenish yellow to yellow with violet markings near the base, June, Switzer-

Top left: Sedum roseum, Roseroot, has greenish-yellow flowers in summer.
This genus can be grown out of doors in temperate climates and many species make attractive rock garden plants.
Centre left: Sempervivum grandiflorum has large starry yellow flowers.
Bottom left: The yellow flowers and greenish-red leaves of Sempervivum ciliosum.
Top right: Sempervivum arachnoideum laggeri has blue-grey rosettes of leaves.
Bottom right: One of the forms of the Common Houseleek.

land. *S. ingwersenii*, dense rosettes flowers pink, edged with white, summer, Caucasus. *S. nevadense*, forms a compact mass of rosettes with small leaves, turning red in summer, flowers red, summer, Spain. *S. tectorum*, St Patrick's cabbage, and numerous other vernacular

names, flattish rosettes 2–3 inches across, sometimes to 8 inches, leaves green, purple-tipped, flowers pinkish-red, July, a very variable species, European Alps. *S. wulfenii*, leaves grey-green, flowers yellow in a hairy panicle, July, central Europe.

Cultivation These are easily grown plants in any light sandy, porous or gritty soil in the sun. Rock gardens, walls, edgings to borders and sink gardens are all suitable places to grow them; even the house roof will suit *S. tectorum* which was once planted on cottage roofs to help to keep the slates in place. Plant from March to June and topdress each spring with well-rotted garden compost or similar material. Propagation is by division or offsets in March, or by seed, but the plants hybridize so freely that it is difficult to be sure of obtaining the required plant by this means.

The Aizoaceae

Argyroderma

From the Greek *argyros*, silver, *derma*, skin, referring to the appearance of the leaves *(Aizoaceae.)* Greenhouse succulents, resembling an oval stone split in half; some species with longer leaves. Flowers are borne singly on a short stalk. There are over 50 species, of which the following are representative of those in cultivation.

Species cultivated *A. aureum*, roundish leaves in pairs, flowers from centre, golden-yellow, Namaqualand. *A. framesii*, flowers pink-purple, Cape Province. *A. luckhoffii*, dwarf, flowers dull yellow, Cape Province. *A. ovale*, makes a small clump, flowers purple-pink, Cape Province. *A. testiculare*, also known as *A. octophyllum*, very pale green, almost white leaves, flowers pink, Karroo.

Cultivation Pot the plants in March in well-drained porous soil; keep on a sunny shelf in the greenhouse or on a sunny window sill. Water well in summer, the growing period, rest without water in winter. Temperature: summer 70°F (21°C), winter not below 40°F (4°C).

Propagation is by seed sown on a good seed compost in deep pans; do not cover the seed. Give plenty of air when germination has taken place as damping-off disease could occur if the atmosphere is too close.

Bergeranthus

Commemorating A. Berger, Curator, Stuttgart Botanic Garden *(Aizoaceae)*. Highly succulent greenhouse plants, making a close group, leaves fairly long and pointed, grey-green, some with small dots. One of the genera included in the group known as mesembryanthemums.

Species cultivated *B. artus*, tapering leaves, flowers yellow, scented, Cape Province. *B. glenensis*, flowers yellow, Orange Free State. *B. multiceps*, long re-curved leaves in clusters, flowers yellow, reddish on outside. Port Elizabeth.

Cultivation Pot in March in compost

Above: Argyroderma aureum, a South African succulent plant with stone-like leaves and golden-yellow flowers.
Below: The flowers of Bergeranthus multiceps, one of the mesembryanthemum group of succulents.

with a few added nutrients, plus $\frac{1}{6}$ part of added coarse sand or grit. Plants grow freely in summer when watering can be as often as the soil dries out. Keep the pots in a sunny position. No water is required in winter when the temperature should not fall below 40°F (4°C). Plants are easy to raise from seed or to increase by cuttings. Sow seed on surface of sandy soil, keep moist but give air when seedlings are above soil.

Carpobrotus

From the Greek *karpos*, fruit, *brotus*, edible, a reference to the edible fruits *(Aizoaceae)*. A genus in the mesembryanthemum group, half-hardy succulent plants, semi-shrubs, their prostrate growths forming clumps. Their leaves are large for the group, curved and three-angled. They have large many-petalled flowers in red, pink, yellow or white.

Species cultivated *C. acinaciformis*, spreading, flowers large, bright carmine, Cape Province, *C. concavus*, thick, glaucous leaves, flowers purple-pink, Cape Province, *C. dimidiatus*, leaves three-angled, flowers pink-purple, Natal. *C. edulis*, the Hottentot fig, often planted at seaside resorts to bind the sand, flowers pink, yellow or yellowish-pink, south west Africa. *C. pillansii*, leaves stiff, sword-shaped, flowers pink-purple, Cape Province. *C. sauerae*, very stout stem with firm sabre-shaped leaves, sharply keeled and curved outwards, flowers large, deep pink, Saldanha Bay.

Cultivation Any well-drained soil is suitable. Plants require little fertilizer. They may be grown in the greenhouse on

Above left: Conophytum, the South African cone plant.
Above: Carpobrotus edulis or Mesembryanthemum edule, the hottentot fig. Naturalized in the milder parts of Britain, the fruits are edible.
Left: Delosperma echinatum, a greenhouse succulent plant from Cape Province.

surrounding the new leaves (*Aizoaceae*). Greenhouse succulents (of the mesembryanthemum group), natives of South Africa, with very thick, fleshy leaves which can dry up and form a sheath over the forming new leaves. Flowers short stalked.

Species cultivated *C. aspera*, rather long, thick leaves, yellow flowers, Namaqualand. *C. bifida*, leaves keeled, thick and flat on top, round below, flowers yellow, Cape Province. *C. candidissima*, long fleshy leaves, flowers golden-yellow, Cape Province. *C. crassa*, leaves short and thick, flowers pale yellow. *C. luckhoffii*, flowers lemon-yellow, Namaqualand. *C. meyeri*, short thick leaves, plants form a mass, flowers large, yellow, Cape Province. *C. peculiaris*, thick leaves which lie flat on the ground, flowers yellow, a splendid species which must be kept quite dry during winter, Cape Province.

Cultivation John Innes potting compost No 1, with a sixth part of added sharp sand, grit and broken brick, makes a suitable compost. Pot in March or April, place in a sunny position in the greenhouse. Water sparingly during early summer then gradually withhold water. Keep plants dry during the winter at a temperature of 45°F (7°C). Any normal greenhouse temperature during summer is sufficient. Propagation is by seed sown on John Innes seed compost in pans in March or when 70°F (21°C) can be maintained. Keep the pans moist and shaded and prick out the seedlings when they are large enough to handle. It is very difficult to increase these plants by cuttings or division.

a sunny shelf or in a rock garden or well-drained border out of doors. Water well in warm weather and keep dry in winter in a minimum temperature of 45°F (7°C). Propagation is by seed as for most mesembryanthemums; do not cover the seed when it is sown. Cuttings will root in equal parts of sand and peat in warm weather. Spray them occasionally to encourage root formation.

Cheiridopsis
From the Greek *cheiris*, a sleeve, *opsis*, like, referring to the withered sheath

Conophytum
From the Greek *konos*, a cone, *phytos*, a plant, referring to the inverted cone

shape of many species *(Aizoaceae)*. Cone plant, pebble plant. Dwarf succulent perennials, spreading to make large clumps; two main types of growth, one roundish, like pebbles, the other with two short lobes on top of a pair of leaves. One of the mesembryanthemum group.

Species cultivated (A selection only), *C. altum*, flowers yellow, *C. batesii*, flowers cream, both from Cape Province. *C. calculus*, flat grey-green bodies, flowers deep yellow, Van Rhynsdorp. *C. divergens*, forms large clumps, flowers white-pink, Cape Province. *C. elishae*, two-lobed type, flowers yellow, Namaqualand. *C. frutescens*, bilobed, flowers deep orange-yellow, Cape Province.

Cultivation Provide a porous soil, such as a compost with few added nutrients, plus a fifth part of coarse sand, grit and broken brick. Pot in August, do not repot often as plants dislike constant moves; water plants according to development. In spring give no water while the skin turns white and dries to a papery substance; when the skin splits start watering and continue until autumn, but never give water in large quantities. Position in full sun; temperature 65–75°F (18–24°C), summer,

50°F (10°C), in winter, but plants can stand a lower temperature in winter if quite dry. Propagation is by seed sown on a good seed compost; do not cover seed, keep moist at 70°F (21°C), shade from sun but give plenty of air when seedlings appear; prick out if seedlings become too crowded or when they are six months old. Plants are also easily increased by breaking off pieces and rooting them in sharp sand.

Delosperma

From the Greek *delos*, conspicuous, *sperma*, seed *(Aizoaceae)*. Greenhouse succulents from South Africa, formerly included in the genus *Mesembryanthemum*, dwarf bushy shrubs, many branched, spreading and prostrate, a few semi-erect, some perennial and others biennial; flowering freely in summer, flowers white, yellow or red. Can be grown out of doors in summer in sunny beds or rock gardens.

Species cultivated *D. angustifolia*, forming a mat 2–3 inches high, leaves narrow, bluish-green, flowers white with pink

Below: Dorotheanthus (Mesembryanthemum) in flower at the Karoo Garden, Worcester, South Africa.

tips, Cape Province. *D. brevisepalum*, compact shrub, flowers white, Cape Province. *D. cooperi*, prostrate growth, flowers purple, Orange Free State. *D. echinatum*, shrub to 1 foot high, thick egg-shaped leaves, white or yellowish, flowers, Cape Province. *D. grandiflorum* erect growth, stems up to 3 feet high, flowers large purple, Cape Province. *D. litorale*, creeping habit, leaves green, edged with white, flowers white, Cape Province. *D. luckhoffii*, dwarf shrub, with dainty branches, flowers pink-purple, Cape Province.

Cultivation These plants will grow well in a soil made from an average potting compost with a fifth part of added roughage. Pot in spring for greenhouse culture, plant out of doors in June, water freely in hot weather but keep dry during winter. Temperatures: 65°F (18°C) in summer; 45°F (7°C) in winter. Plants may be raised from seed or increased by cuttings; the cuttings soon make roots and can flower soon after.

Dorotheanthus

Named in honour of Frau Dorothea Schwantes, wife of a German botanist *(Aizoaceae)*. Greenhouse succulents from South Africa, often found under

Mesembryanthemum. They may be used for bedding out or as pot plants.

Species cultivated *D. bellidiformis*, dwarf spreading plant, leaves fleshy, flowers open in sunshine, colours, white, pink, red and orange. *D. gramineus*, short-stemmed and spreading, flowers bright carmine. *D. tricolor*, spreading habit, leaves long and curved, flowers white below and purple above. All these are natives of Cape Province.

Cultivation An open compost is needed; out of doors see that the soil is well drained and plant in sunny positions. These plants are annuals and three plants in a pot make a good display; they do not require high temperatures. Propagation is by seeds sown on a good seed compost. Do not cover the seed. The temperature should be 70°F (21°C). Keep the seed pans moist and shaded while germination is taking place, prick out the seedlings and grow them on in a frame. The plants should be potted up or planted out in June.

Drosanthemum

From *Drosera* (the sundew) and the Greek *anthemon*, flower *(Aizoaceae)*. Greenhouse succulent shrubs, of the *Mesembryanthemum* group, with erect or prostrate stems, leaves three-angled to cylindrical, covered with sparkling papillae (tiny, pimple-like protuberances) reminiscent of the dew-like glands on the leaves of the sundew (*Drosera*), hence the derivation of the name. The flowers open in the afternoon in sunshine.

Species cultivated *D. albiflorum*, dainty shrub, about 6 inches high, flowers white, Cape Province. *D. bicolor*, erect stiff stems, up to 1 foot high, flowers purple with a golden-yellow centre, Little Karoo. *D. hispidum*, shrub up to 2 feet high, leaves thick and fleshy, flowers deep purple, very free-flowering and handsome, South West Africa.

Cultivation Drosanthemums should be provided with a very porous soil, consisting of a compost with few added nutrients to which has been added a fifth part of coarse sand, grit, broken brick and granulated charcoal. They are easy to grow; plants should be out of doors during the summer and in a frost-free greenhouse in the winter. Propagation is by seeds or cuttings; seeds are small and should not be covered. Moisture and warmth soon brings seedlings along and they will flower the first year. Cuttings soon strike in an equal mixture of peat and sharp sand; spray them occasionally.

Faucaria

From the Latin *fauces*, the throat, a reference to the open, throat-like appearance of the pairs of leaves *(Aizoaceae)*. A genus of succulent plants of the *Mesembryanthemum* group, for the greenhouse or a sunny window. They are almost stemless, with crowded fleshy

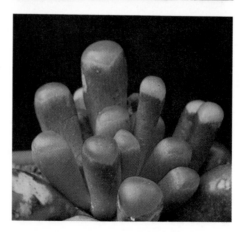

Top: Drosanthemum hispidum grows to 0.6m (2 feet) and comes from Cape Province.
Centre: Faucaria tuberculosa, from South Africa, has fleshy triangular leaves.
Bottom: Fenestraria aurantiaca, the Window Plant, has a clear top to its leaves.

leaves which curve up at the edges and carry soft, thorn-like projections on the sides.

Species cultivated *F. albidens*, leaves boat-shaped, toothed at edges, flowers yellow, South Africa. *F. felina*, fleshy leaves with pronounced teeth at the edges, flowers golden-yellow, Cape Province. *F. lupina*, keeled leaf with teeth, flowers yellow, Port Elizabeth. *F. tigrina*, tiger's claw, very thick leaves, flowers golden-yellow, Cape Province. *F. tuberculosa*, leaves triangular, very thick, upper surface warted, teeth few, flowers yellow, South Africa.

Cultivation Pot these plants in a regular potting compost, with a sixth part of sand, grit or broken brick. Repot every two years or when the plant reaches the side of the pot. Water from March to September, but keep dry in winter. If plants are kept in a heated room in winter, water them once a month. During the growing season, when plants are watered regularly, the temperature can rise to 65°F (18°C), but can be allowed to fall to 45–50°F (7–10°C), in winter. The plants should be in a light position but need not have strong sunshine. They are easily raised from seed sown in pans of a good seed compost in March. Keep moist, shaded and at 70°F (21°C). Seedlings grow quickly and can flower when they are a year old. Large plants can be broken up and the offsets rooted in sharp sand.

Fenestraria

From the Latin *fenestra*, a window-referring to the transparent, window, like patch of skin on top of the stem (*Aizoaceae*). A genus of two species, small succulent plants from South Africa, belonging to the *Mesembryanthemum* group. They make groups of small pebble-like stems with a patch of clear skin at the top. When the plant is almost covered with sand as it is in its native habitat, the clear top allows sunlight to penetrate to the chlorophyll in the leaves.

Species cultivated *F. aurantiaca*, small club-shaped leaves, flat at the top, flowers on short stalks in August, golden-yellow, Cape Province. *F. rhopalophylla*, similar to preceding plant, but leaves shorter, flowers white, Southwest Africa.

Cultivation These little plants should be grown in an average potting compost, with a seventh part added of coarse sand, grit and broken brick. Repot every four years in April, water sparingly from March to September, keep dry in winter. The pots should be given the sunniest place in the greenhouse: temperature, 65–85°F (18–29°C), in summer, 45°F (7°C), in winter. Propagation is by seed sown on a good seed compost; the seed must not be covered. Sow in pans in March at a temperature of 70°F (21°C), keep moist and shaded, do not hurry pricking out; the seedlings can remain in the pan until the following spring. Plants may also be divided and the small pieces rooted.

Gibbaeum

From the Latin *gibba*, a hump, a reference to the humped appearance of one of each pair of leaves (*Aizoaceae*). Greenhouse succulent plants forming large clumps, from South Africa, mainly the Little Karoo, belonging to the *Mesembryanthemum* group, having short stems and thick, fleshy leaves, some species with pairs of leaves of differing lengths.

Species cultivated *G. album*, leaves short and thick, flowers white, or rose pink, Little Karoo. *G. dispar*, leaves have very short papillae, giving a velvety feel and appearance to the plant, flowers pink, Ladysmith Division, *G. gibbosum*. pairs of very unequal length leaves, longer leaf incurved, flowers pale pink with purple mid-stripe. *G. heathii*, pairs of leaves almost round and close together, flowers cream turning pink, Cape Province. *G. pubescens*, thick, rather longer leaves than some species and of unequal length, flowers violet-red, Ladysmith Division. *G. shandii*, very similar to *G. pubescens* only difference being that the green epidermis shows through the hairs on *G. shandii* but not on *G. pubescens*. *G. velutinum*, fleshy, keeled leaves, making a small clump, flowers white or pale pink, Little Karoo. This is a winter growing species which needs a minimum winter temperature of 55°F (13°C).

Cultivation Use a compost with few added nutrients with a sixth part added of roughage in the form of coarse sand, grit and broken brick. Repot every two years, in March. Give the plants a position on a sunny shelf in the greenhouse. Water sparingly at all times during the growing period; keep quite dry from September to March. Temperatures should be 65–75°F (18–24°C) in the growing season and 45°F (7°C), in winter. Propagation is by seeds sown on a good seed compost; do not cover seed. Keep at 70°F (21°C), moist and shaded. Offshoots may also be detached, dried off and rooted in sand and peat in equal parts.

Glottiphyllum

From the Greek *glotta*, tongue, *phyllon*

leaf, referring to the leaf shape (*Aizoaceae*). Greenhouse succulent plants belonging to the Mesembryanthemum group, with very fleshy leaves on short stems, making groups. They produce rather large flowers on short stems, in summer. Plants are self-sterile but hybridise easily.

Species cultivated *G. album*, white flowers, Cape Province, *G. depressum*, yellow flowers, South Africa. *G. fragrans*, flowers golden-yellow, scented, Cape Province. *G. marlothii*, flowers golden-yellow, very free flowering, Karoo.

Cultivation An average potting compost,

Top: Gibbaeum album is a South African succulent plant forming large clumps of fleshy leaves.
Left centre: A yellow-flowered hybrid Lampranthus.
Right centre: Glottiphyllum velutinum has groups of fleshy leaves typical of the genus.
Bottom left: Lampranthus aurantiacus.
Bottom right: The yellow Mesembryanthemum-like flowers of Glottiphyllum davisii are representative of all the species.

with a fifth part added of coarse sand, grit and broken brick is suitable; pots must be well drained and placed in sunny positions. Plants grow from April to the end of June, when the pots or pans can be placed out of doors in a sunny position, protected from excess of rain. Water only during the growing season and when soil has dried out completely or the plants will become too soft; keep dry in winter. If given dry conditions and full sun plants will become pink or red. Temperature, October to February, 45°F (7°C), March to October 55°F (13°C), or over. Propagation is by seed sown on a good seed compost; do not cover seed; keep moist, shaded and at a temperature of 70°F (21°C). Plants can be divided easily to increase specimens.

Lampranthus

From the Greek *lampros*, bright, and *anthos*, flower; the flowers are very showy (*Aizoaceae*). Greenhouse succulent plants, sub-shrubs with spreading branches and thick leaves, mostly small and of varying shapes, and mostly from South Africa. The flowers are borne prolifically throughout the summer, in white, pink, rose, red, purple, orange or yellow and the plants are ideal for outdoor beds, or rock gardens. They grow well on windowsills.

Species cultivated *L. aurantiacus*, compact shrubby plant to 3 feet, orange flowers, Cape Province. *L. aureus*, 1½ feet, fleshy angled leaves, orange flowers, Cape Province. *L. blandus*, 1½ feet, leaves angled and covered with fine dots, pink flowers, Port Alfred. *L. brownii*, 1 foot, grey-green leaves, flowers yellow to orange, then to light red, Cape Province. *L. coccineus*, 2½ feet, small, blunt, angled leaves, bright red flowers, Cape Province. *L. spectabilis*, prostrate, a beautiful flowering plant with masses of purple flowers, Cape Province. Other species with similar flowers, in various colours, are grown out of doors in the milder areas of Britain, Canada and the north U.S., where frosts are infrequent.

Cultivation A regular potting compost is suitable with ⅙ part added of coarse material in the form of sharp sand, grit and broken brick. Pot in March and place in a sunny position in the greenhouse. Plant out from early June to September in a sunny position and water freely between April and September, but keep dry in winter. The minimum winter temperature should be 40°F (4°C) and in summer ordinary seasonal warmth is satisfactory. Propagate by seed sown in a good seed compost in March in a temperature of 70°F (21°C), keep shaded and moist. Propagate also by cuttings which root easily in sharp sand. Choose stems which have not become woody and let the cuttings dry at the base before inserting in sand. Spray occasionally.

Lithops

From the Greek *lithos*, a stone, and *ops*, appearance, in reference to the resemblance of these plants to stones (*Aizoaceae*). Pebble plants, living stones. The lithops are succulent greenhouse plants from South Africa, never more than an inch high, but making large groups with age. They consist of a pair of leaves

Top: Lithops kuibesebsis has yellow flowers.
Below: L. erniana is daisy-like.
Lithops can be looked after better when grown in colonies.

joined half way up or completely, leaving only a small slit on the surface. The top is almost flat and many species having markings similar to some bird's eggs. Flowers are either white or yellow, the yellow varieties flower in July and August, the white from September to November.

Species cultivated *L. aucampiae*, a fine plant with large bodies, almost brick red, Transvaal. *L. bella*, well-marked plant body white flowers, south-west Africa. *L. bromfieldii*, rather brown with many markings, Cape Province. *L. christinae*, grey-blue body, south-west Africa. *L. de boeri*, well mottled face to bodies. *L. dorotheae*, very handsome with distinct markings, Bushmanland. *L. fulleri*, grey with brown markings, Little Namaqualand. *L. leslei*, green face with reddish spots, Transvaal. It is worth noting that many species are thought by some specialists to be varieties only.

Cultivation A very porous compost is required; an average potting compost with $\frac{1}{4}$ part added of roughage, consisting of coarse sharp sand, or grit, broken brick and granulated charcoal, is suitable. Repotting is required every three years, in May or June, or when the plant reaches the side of the pot. A winter minimum temperature of 40°F (4°C) is required; in summer the normal seasonal temperature within the greenhouse suits them. They do not need shade. Do not water in the early part of the year. New plants form inside the old pair of leaves, these leaves being absorbed until only a paperlike skin is left to protect the new plant, and no water must be given until the old leaves have dried up. Then water carefully up to November, and give very little in December. No exact time can be given for starting watering after the resting period, as the species differ considerably as to when water is needed.

Propagate by seed, which need only be sown on the top of the compost. A good seed compost, sifted through a perforated zinc sieve can be used. Place the coarsest particles over the crocks, then cover with unsifted compost, and finish the top inch with the finest particles from sifting. Sow in March in a temperature of 70–80°F (21–27°C) and shade from sun, but give light until the seedlings appear. Propagate also by division, by cutting off individual heads with a small piece of stem attached.

Mesembryanthemum

From the Greek *mesos*, middle, *embryon*, fruit, and *anthemon*, flower; not from *mesembria*, mid-day and *anthemob*, as is usually suggested. The earliest species known flowered at mid-day, but when night flowering species were discovered the name was changed to give a change of sense without a change of sound (*Aizoaceae*). These are greenhouse succulent plants, many suitable for bedding out for the summer with a creeping habit of growth, fleshy leaves and brilliant coloured flowers.

Species cultivated *M. albatum*, branch-

Mesembryanthemums are useful for providing colourful summer bedding.

ing, green and pinkish-red flowers, Cape Province. *M. crystallinum*, ice plant, spreading branches, white flowers, south-west Africa. *M. fulleri*, annual, white flowers, Cape Province. *M. intranspurens*, erect stem, white and pink flowers, Cape Province. *M. macrophyllum* prostrate, violet-pink flowers, Nemaqualand *M. nodiflorum*, cylindrical leaves, white flowers, Africa, the Middle East and California. *M. setosum*, pink and greenish flowers, Cape Province. *M. striatum*, prostrate, white flowers, Cape Province. The plant popularly known as *M. criniflorum* is now called *Dorotheanthus criniflorum*.

Cultivation They should be grown in a very porous soil, such as a compost with few added nutrients with $\frac{1}{4}$ part added of coarse sand, grit, broken brick and granulated charcoal. The greenhouse kinds require a sunny position, with plenty of ventilation in hot weather. Give them a minimum winter tem-

perature of 45°F (7°C), and normal greenhouse temperature during summer. Water only when the soil has dried out and keep dry during the winter. Propagate from seed sown in a good seed compost in March in a temperature of 65–70°F (18–21°C). Do not cover the seed, but keep it moist and shaded until the seedlings are pricked out. Also by cuttings taken during the summer and rooted in equal parts of sharp sand and peat. These can then be put out in a sunny position in well-drained soil as bedding plants, or on a rock garden.

Neohenricia

Derivation uncertain (*Aizoaceae*). A small genus of greenhouse succulent plants belonging to the *Mesembryanthemum* group. They have very small leaves, about $\frac{1}{4}$ inch long, opposite, eventually forming a dense mat. The tips of the leaves have very small warts. Very sweet smelling flowers, about $\frac{1}{4}$ inch in diameter, are formed on short stems, opening at night.

The only species cultivated is *N*.

sibbetii, the leaves of which turn dark purple in full sunshine. It is a native of the Orange Free State.

Cultivation The compost should consist of an average compost with a ¼ part added of coarse sand, grit or broken brick. A sunny position in the greenhouse is required at all times. Water from March to September taking care not to allow water to remain around the neck of the rosettes. In winter keep the plants dry and maintain a minimum temperature of 45°F (7°C).

Propagation is by division of the mats or by seed sown in a good seed compost, kept moist and shaded at a temperature of 70°F (21°C) until seedlings appear, when more light should be allowed. Prick out the seedlings when they are large enough to handle.

Ophthalmophyllum

From the Greek *ophthalmos*, eye, and *phyllon*, leaf, in reference to the clear skin on top of the leaves through which the plant receives light, which it might not otherwise get (*Aizoaceae*). These are succulent plants for the greenhouse from South Africa. They are curious-looking plants in that they consist of a pair of very thick fleshy leaves fused together except for a slit down the centre from which the flowers come. They are often referred to as window plants, owing to the colourless skin on the upper leaf surface which allows light to reach into the plant when most of it is covered with sand. All ophthalmophyllums are very similar in appearance, and with some of them, the bodies of the plants turn red when exposed to full sun.

Species cultivated *O. dinteri*, looks like a lithops, except that the top is transparent without markings, flowers violet-red. *O. pubescens*, short thick pairs of leaves, white to pink flowers, Cape Province. *O. schlecteri*, almost round plants, white flowers, Little Namaqualand.

Cultivation Use a compost with few added nutrients with ⅕ part added of sand, grit and broken brick. Pot them in summer and place them in the sunniest position in the greenhouse. Their main growing period is July–November, and during their resting period the old leaves dry up and protect the new ones, which burst through the dry skins. Afterwards the plants flower. From January to July they should be kept quite dry, and when growth begins, watered only sparingly. If too much water is given, the plants will burst their bodies. Give them a temperature of 50°F (10°C) in winter, and 80°F (27°C) in summer. Propagate during April by seed sown on a good seed compost (the seed should not be covered). Keep the pans moist, shaded and at a temperature of 70°F (21°C.) Seedlings must be kept dry between November and March. Plants do not make a group very quickly and it is not advisable to break them up to increase stock. A fine specimen

could well be ruined in this way if it is broken up in this way.

Oscularia

From the Latin *osculum*, a little mouth, for no apparent reason (*Aizoaceae*). Part of the *Mesembryanthemum* family these greenhouse succulents, of which there are 5 species, can be planted out of doors

Above: A pan of Ophthalmophyllum herrei, a succulent from South Africa. The leaves allow light to enter the skin. Left: Oscularia caulescens.

in the summer. They are small shrubby plants with thick, angled leaves, natives of Cape Province, South Africa.

Species cultivated *Oscularia caulescens*, shrubby, reddish stems, leaves thick, pointed and with two or three small teeth on the edges, small, pink fragrant flowers, summer. *O. deltoides*, branching shrub with reddish stems, short thick grey leaves with small reddish teeth on the edges, numerous pale pink flowers, summer.

Cultivation Use a mixture of an average potting compost with ⅙ part of roughage added, and pot the plants in March. When the plants are kept in the greenhouse, they should be watered only when the soil dries out. Keep them in a temperature of about 65°F (18°C) in the growing season, but in winter do not let the temperature fall below 45°F (7°C).

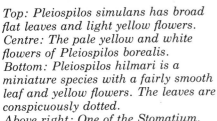

Top: Pleiospilos simulans has broad flat leaves and light yellow flowers.
Centre: The pale yellow and white flowers of Pleiospilos borealis.
Bottom: Pleiospilos hilmari is a miniature species with a fairly smooth leaf and yellow flowers. The leaves are conspicuously dotted.
Above right: One of the Stomatium, with toothed leaves like open mouths.

They can be planted out of doors between June and September in well-drained soil and a sunny position. Propagation is by seed sown in March on reliable seed compost, in a temperature of 65–70°F (18–21°C). The seed should not be covered, but the seed boxes or pans should be kept moist until the seeds have germinated and the seedlings are large enough to handle, when they should be pricked off into individual small pots and kept in somewhat drier conditions. Alternatively, stem cuttings root quickly in a mixture of sharp sand and peat and will flower in their first season.

Pleiospilos

From the Greek *pleios*, full, and *spilos*, a dot or spot, in reference to the conspicuous spotting of the leaves (*Aizoaceae*). A genus of greenhouse succulent perennials which belong to the *Mesembryanthemum* group, natives of Cape Province. The growth consists mainly of two pairs of leaves, very fleshy, with one pair forming and the other withering. They are stemless and often resemble pieces of rock or granite. There are about 38 species. They are sometimes referred to as living stones, a name also applied to the related *Lithops*.

Species cultivated *P. bolusii*, rough grey leaves looking like pieces of granite, golden-yellow flowers from the centre of a pair of leaves. *P. dekanahi*, long grey-green leaves, flowers pale yellow. *P. hilmari*, miniature, fairly smooth leaf, yellow flowers. *P. minor*, short, thick, triangular leaves, yellow flowers. *P. nelii*, almost round leaves, pinkish-yellow flowers in early spring. *P. simulans*, broad flat leaves, light yellow to orange flowers.

Cultivation Grow these succulents in a compost with few added nutrients with $\frac{1}{5}$ part added of sand, grit and broken brick; limestone chippings can be used instead of the brick. Pot in May every two years and give them as sunny a position as possible. Water only when the old pair of leaves has almost dried up, and do not give any water at all after August. During the winter they require a minimum temperature of 45°F (7°C), and in the growing period will thrive in the usual greenhouse temperature. Propagation is by seed sown in March in pans of a good seed compost; leave the seed uncovered, keep it moist and shaded in a temperature of 70°F (21°C) and the seedlings will flower in the second year. They may also be propagated from cuttings obtained from divided clumps; use deep pots as most species have long roots.

Stomatium

From the Greek *stoma*, mouth; the pairs of toothed leaves look like an open mouth (*Aizoaceae*). A genus of 40 species of greenhouse succulent plants of the *Mesembryanthemum* group. The plants form dense clumps of rosettes made up of opposite thick leaves of unequal length on very short, thick stems. The leaves usually have short, blunt teeth along their edges and very small tubercles on the leaf surface. The flowers are golden-yellow, open at night and are produced in summer. They are natives of Cape Province.

Species cultivated *S. ermininum*, leaves about 1 inch long, triangular at the tip, and keeled. *S. fulleri*, six leaves on each head, tips recurved. *S. peersii*, leaves

Above: Stapelia flavirostris.
Left: Kleinia fulgens (inset: a floret enlarged), a succulent from Natal, suitable for the cool greenhouse.

takes place, then admit more light. Transplant the seedlings when large enough to handle. Flowering plants can be had in the second year. Cuttings taken from mature plants can be rooted in a mixture of coarse sand and peat.

The Asclepiadaceae

Stapelia
Commemorating J. B. van Stapel, a Dutch physician of the seventeenth century (*Asclepiadaceae*). Carrion flower. A genus of 75 species of greenhouse succulent perennials with fleshy stems shaped like stag's horns. The flowers are 5-petalled, some with hairs; many have a foul smell. This attracts blow-flies which pollinate the flowers. Any maggots which hatch from the flies' eggs quickly die since there is no food for them in the flowers. The plants are natives of semi-arid regions of tropical Africa and South Africa.
Species cultivated *S. asterias*, starfish flower, to 10 inches, flowers dark purple and pale yellow, summer, Karoo. *S. gettleffii*, flowers yellow and purple, Transvaal. *S. gigantea*, flowers yellow with crimson lines, to 10 inches across, pointed petals, Cape Province. *S. variegata*, most commonly cultivated, fleshy stems, flower colour very variable, but basically yellow with red spots, August, Cape Province.
Cultivation Use an average potting compost with more sand, if necessary, to make it sufficiently porous. Pot every year in March, removing the old growth, as the plants flower best on the new growth. Water well between March and September as long as the pots are well drained. Care should be taken to ensure that no stagnant moisture forms at the neck of the plants. In winter just enough water should be given to

prevent shrivelling. The minimum temperature in winter should be 50°F (10°C), and in summer between 65–75°F (18–24°C). Ventilation in winter should be good as otherwise black mould may form on the plants. Propagation is by seed sown in a good seed compost in March at a temperature of 70°F (21°C). The seeds can germinate in 48 hours; prick out the seedlings when they are two months old or they may rot off. Plants may also be propagated by cuttings of new growths, dried and inserted lightly into sand. Do not push them into the sand or they may rot off.

The Compositae and Euphorbiaceae

Euphorbia
Named after Euphorbus, physician to King Juba of Mauritania (*Euphorbiaceae*). A genus of about a thousand species, widely distributed, mainly in temperate regions, showing immense diversity of form and requirements. They include annual, biennial and perennial herbaceous plants, shrubs and trees and succulent plants. The decorative parts are really bracts, often colourful, round the small and inconspicuous flowers. Some are warm greenhouse plants others are hardy. The succulent species are mainly from Africa, most of them from South and West Africa. Many of those resemble cacti in appearance. All euphorbias exude a poisonous milky latex when the stems are cut, which can burn the skin and eyes and which, in some species, is poisonous if taken internally.
Succulent There are very many species in cultivation; some of the following are some of the more popular ones, *E. alcicornis*, to 2 feet, leafless, spiny shrub, stem five angled, Malagasy. *E. bupleurifolia*, dwarf, thick stem like a tight fir cone, large deciduous plant growing from the top, pale green flowers, Cape Province. *E. canariensis*, shrub with small yellow flowers, many erect stems, 4–6 ribbed, short spines on edges, Canary Isles. *E. caput-medusae*, dwarf, thick main stem, making a large head from which radiate many thin branches a foot or more long, small yellow flowers. There is a cristate or monstrous form with thin, flattened branches, Cape Province. *E. echinus*, shrub with erect stem and many branches, 5–8 angled, stems similar in shape to the cactus, *Cereus eburneus*, south Morocco. *E. obesa*, one of the most popular euphorbias, plants round when young, coloured like plaid, becoming columnar, closely resembling the cactus, *Astrophytum asterias;* this plant does not make offsets so must be grown from seed, Cape Province. *E. splendens*, crown of thorns, 2–3 feet, succulent, spiny, few-leaved shrub, pairs of round scarlet bracts, mainly in spring, Malagasy.

very short, thick and pointed. *S. suaveolens*, leaves very thick, about ¾ inch long, turning red when grown in full sun.
Cultivation The compost should consist of an average potting compost to which has been added ½ part of coarse sand, grit or broken brick. A light position in the greenhouse is required. In summer keep the compost moist; flowering takes place about July. In winter keep the soil dry and maintain a minimum temperature of 45°F (7°C). Propagation is by seed sown in a good seed compost and kept moist and shaded at 70°F (21°C) until germination

Top left: Euphorbia obesa, a succulent has distinguishing plaid-like markings.
Top right: The Partridge-breasted Aloe Aloe variegata.
Above: Aloe candelabrum.

Cultivation Most of these plants like a richer soil than some succulents but it must be porous. The compost should be made up from an average potting compost with a fifth part added of sharp sand, grit or broken brick. Repot in March every two years or when the plants become pot-bound; water well from April to September, keep fairly dry from October to March. Temperatures should be 65°F (18°C), in the growing period, 45–50°F (7–10°C) in winter. Plants should be given a light sunny place in the greenhouse, or on a window sill. Propagation is by seed sown in early spring in pans of reliable seed compost. Cover the seed with its own depth of soil, keep moist at temperature of 70°F (21°C), shade from sun but give light when seedlings appear. Large seeds should be washed well before sowing. Plants may also be propagated by cuttings which should be dusted with powdered charcoal to prevent bleeding, then dried and rooted in sharp sand and peat in equal parts. Pot up the cuttings, when they have rooted, in the compost described above.

Kleinia

Commemorating Dr J. Th. Klein, 1685–1759, a German botanist (*Compositae*). These are succulent greenhouse perennials, mostly with fleshy stems, some with cylindrical leaves. Some authorities have transferred the genus to *Senecio*.

Species cultivated *K. articulata*, thick cylindrical stems with temporary leaves, yellowish flowers, evil-smelling, winter, known as the candle plant, Cape Province. *K. fulgens*, 1–2 feet, large tuberous root, leaves covered with pale violet wax flowers red, May, Natal. *K. galpinii*, 1½ feet, shrub or semi-shrub, orange-red, October, Transvaal. *K. mandraliscae*, fleshy stem, loose procumbent growth, S. Africa. *K. neriifolia*, 3 feet, shrubby thick fleshy stems, creamy flowers, autumn, Canary Islands, *K. pendula*, stems often bend over and re-enter soil to root themselves, red, autumn, S. Arabia. *K. repens*, 8–12 inches, narrow leaves, white flowers, summer, Cape Province. *K. stapeliiformis*, shrubby, tall erect stems shaped like stapelia stems, red flowers on long stalks, May–June, E. Africa. *K. tomentosa*, 1 foot, shrubby, long, thick, cylindrical leaves covered with white felt, yellow flowers, July, south-west Africa.

Cultivation Use a compost with few additions plus $\frac{1}{6}$ part of sharp sand, grit and broken brick, and pot in spring in well-drained pots. Kleinias prefer a sunny place in the greenhouse or a sunny window, with a winter temperature of 40–45°F (4–7°C) and a normal greenhouse temperature in the summer. Watering should be once a month in winter, and between March and September, as often as the soil dries out. They can be planted outside when all danger of frost has gone. Propagate by cuttings dried and then rooted in sharp sand, between June and August.

The Liliaceae

Aloe

The Greek name, or from the Arabic *alloch* (*Liliaceae*). Evergreen plants for greenhouse and window; some are small and suitable for room culture, others grow very tall and tree like. There are very many species and they have leaves in the form of rosettes, some are strongly toothed at the edges, others are smooth. The leaves in some species are large and leathery and others are striped with yellow markings.

Species cultivated As there are hundreds of species and varieties it is possible to name only a few. *A. abyssinica*, stemless, many leaves in rosettes, sword-shaped and strongly toothed, flowers numerous on tall stalks, red-yellow, Eritrea. *A. africana*, stem 6 feet high, leaves in rosettes, tough and spiny, flowers yellow to orange, Transvaal, Port Elizabeth,

Above left: Agave americana marginata is sometimes used as a dot plant in summer bedding.
Above right: Agave parviflora.
Left: Gasteria armstrongii a greenhouse succulent plant from Cape Province.

ridge, flowers bell shaped on tall stem, greenish pink easily propagated by suckers sent up from below ground level, Namaqualand, Cape Province.

Cultivation A suitable compost consists of 2 parts of loam, 1 part of peat, 1 part of very sharp, coarse sand (river grit is best), to which should be added a good base fertilizer as a compost with few added nutrients. Grow the plants in a sunny greenhouse in pots or tubs, large tubs may be stood outside greenhouse for summer. Water when soil is dry during April to September, but refrain when the weather is cold and dull; give winter's rest. Pot in March or April. Temperature: winter, 45–50°F (7–10°C), summer to 65°F (18°C). Propagation is by seeds or offsets, some species by leaf cuttings. Seed should be sown in early spring in reliable seed compost, just covering the seed in a temperature of 70°F (21°C) for in lower temperatures seed is slow to germinate.

Gasteria

From the Greek *gaster*, belly, an allusion to the swollen flower base (*Liliaceae*). Greenhouse succulent plants, almost stemless, leaves leathery and mostly warted and mottled in colour. Leaves usually opposite one another, but some species form rosettes with age. Favourite plants for greenhouse or window culture.

Port Alfred. *A. arborescens*, grows very tall (20–30 feet), makes many stems in clump, leaves horny and toothed, purple-red flowers, Cape Province. *A. aristata*, compact rosettes, very thin, pointed leaves, lightly toothed and speckled with white, orange-red flowers, Cape Province, Natal, Orange Free State, can winter out of doors in mild northern areas. *A. candelabrum*, tree like, stems bare low down with some dried leaves adhering near top, leaves recurved in rosettes, scarlet or orange-pink flowers, Natal, Durban. *A. claviflora*, stemless, leaves in clusters, sword-shaped and upcurved, yellowish-orange-red flowers, Bushmanland. *A. comosa*, tree-like, greenish-white flowers, Cape Province. *A. davyiana*, stemless, leaves fleshy with reddish spots on upper surface, pale pink flowers, Transvaal. *A. dichotoma*, grows to 40 feet or more, stem bare with cluster of leaves at top, bright yellow flowers, Little Namaqualand. *A. variegata*, the well known partridge-breasted aloe, a very good house plant, triangular-shaped pointed leaves, pale green with darker markings like feathers of part-

All have flowers like small bells on a tall stalk, greenish-pink in colour.

Species cultivated There are many in cultivation and some are difficult to identify as differences are small. There are also many inter specific hybrids as well as inter generic hybrids. *G. armstrongii*, very short, thickened leaves in pairs from centre of plant, flowers reddish-green, Cape Province. *G. disticha*, dark green leaves spotted with white, Cape Province. *G. liliputana*, smallest of the Gasterias, leaves spirally arranged, dark green, spotted white, freely off-setting, flowers red, Cape Province. *G. maculata*, tongue-like leaves, well marked with white blotches, freely off-setting from the base, Cape Province. *G. nigricans*, thick green leaves incurved and spotted, Port Elizabeth. *G. trigona*, long, tongue-like leaves, pointed, freely off-setting, Cape Province. *G. verrucosa*, leaves very long, opposite, dark green with many white tubercles, forms groups, Cape Province.

Cultivation Use a compost with few added nutrients with a sixth part added of coarse sand, grit and broken brick. Place the pots on a sunny shelf in spring but give slight shade during the hotter months of the year. Pot in March or April, water when the soil dries out from April to September, but keep dry from October to March. Propagation is mainly by removing offsets or by taking leaf cuttings. Seed is not recommended due to the ease with which hybrids form. If seed is used it should be sown in a good seed compost, just covering the seed with sifted compost. Keep moist and shaded at a temperature of 70°F (21°C).

The Agavaceae and Amyrrilidaceae

Agave

From the Greek *agaros*, admirable (*Agavaceae*). Succulent plants, from the warmer regions of the Western Hemisphere, a large genus comprising herbs, semi-shrubs or shrubs, some of economic importance; from one species the fibre sisal is produced. Leaves fleshy, sword shaped, often with spikes at their tips, some dagger shaped, others split off in shreds at the edges, always forming rosettes. Some are grown out of doors in milder northern districts, and particularly fine specimens can be seen in Britain at Tresco, Isles of Scilly. Their flowers are borne on tall spikes up to 30–40 feet high. The small flowers are mostly reddish green. The rosettes of most species die after seed has ripened but offsets are produced, except by *A. horrida*.

Species cultivated *A. albicans*, 3–4 feet, Mexico. *A. americana* (American aloe, century plant, so called because it was once thought that it took plants 100 years to flower. In fact, plants may flower after 10 years.) Spectacular flower spikes 30–40 feet tall, Mexico; vars. *marginata*, yellowish-white or deep yellow edges to leaves, *medio-picta*, yellow central stripe, *striata*, yellow or white lines on leaves, *variegata*, with dark green and yellow twisted leaves. *A. angustifolia*, leaves 2 feet long, 3 inches wide, flower spike to 8 feet high, Central America. *A. atrovirens*, leaves 6 feet long, 1 foot wide, spike 20–30 feet, South Mexico. *A. decipiens*, spike up to 40 feet high, 4 feet long, 4 inches wide, with sharp teeth on the edges, flowers greenish yellow, South America. *A. horrida*, leaves 8 feet high, rosettes 2 feet across, Mexico. *A. parviflora*, dwarf species with thick, fleshy leaves, 3–4 inches long, split into white threads at the ends, greenish-white flowers on a spike to 5 feet tall, S. Arizona.

Cultivation The compost should be very porous; a compost with few added nutrients, with $\frac{1}{6}$ part of added roughage consisting of very coarse sand or broken brick and charcoal is suitable. Position, large pots or tubs in greenhouse. Plants will benefit from being placed outdoors during the summer. Water during late spring, summer and early autumn, only when the soil is almost dry. Do not pot too often, every five or six years is enough. Summer temperatures up to 70°F (21°C), winter 50°F (10°C). Propagation is by offsets potted in sharp sand till rooted, or by seed sown in a good seed compost.

Beschorneria

Named for F. W. C. Beschorner, a German botanist (*Amaryllidaceae*). A small genus of Mexican plants allied to *Agave* and usually treated as greenhouse evergreen succulents.

Species cultivated *B. bracteata*, 5–6 feet, flowers opening green in March becoming yellowish-red as they mature. *B. dekosteriana*, 8 feet, flowers green, tinged red, February. *B. tubiflora*, 3 feet, flowers reddish-green, February. *B. yuccoides*, 5–6 feet, flowers bright green with rosy-red bracts, May and June. This species may be grown in the open in well-drained soil and a sunny position in mild northern areas.

Cultivation Beschornerias require a well-drained sandy compost with mortar rubble and loam. A minimum winter temperature of about 55°F (13°C) should be maintained. Very little water is required during the winter months and plants should be watered only moderately from April to August. Plants may be stood in the open from June to early September. Propagate by offsets detached and inserted in pots at almost any time.

The Vitaceae and Portulaceae

Cissus

From the Greek *kissos*, ivy (*Vitaceae*). Greenhouse perennials; some species climbing with very thick stems, some slender-stemmed climbers, some forming a large base (known as caudex) similar to a huge corm; flowers borne in racemes or umbels.

Succulent species cultivated *C. bainesii*, thick bottle-shaped caudex, leaves notched, flowers in racemes, greenish and small, South-West Africa. *C. juttae*, very thick caudex branching stems, leaves pointed-oval, interesting to raise from seed, South-West Africa. *C. rotundifolia*, climbing plant with four-angled stem, flowers green, small, berries red, Tanzania.

Cultivation For the succulent species provide a very porous soil, a sandy loam with broken brick to increase porosity; repot the plants in March, not more often than every three years, keeping the corm at the old soil level; water sparingly in summer and not at all in winter; provide a sunny position, with a temperature of 65–75°F (18–24°C) in summer, 45°F (7°C) in winter, when plants should be kept quite dry. Propagation of succulent species is by seeds sown in reliable seed compost in a warm position; they are very slow to germinate; also by pieces of stem which can be encouraged to root in a compost of sharp sand and peat in equal proportions.

Portulaca

An old Latin name, possibly from the Latin *porto*, to carry, and *lac*, milk, in allusion to the milky juice (*Portulacaceae*). These are succulent annual and perennial herbaceous plants, with fibrous or thickened roots and small fleshy leaves. Of the 200 or more species in this genus, widespread in tropical and sub-tropical regions, many are con-

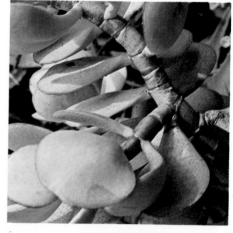

sidered to be weeds and the group is not very important for garden cultivation. The leaves of *P. oleracea* can be used in salads.

Species cultivated *P. grandiflora*, annual stems procumbent and spreading, flowers white, yellow, pink, red or orange, June–July, Brazil. *P. lutea*, coarse-stemmed perennial, yellow flowers, summer, Pacific Islands. *P. oleracea*, purslane, annual, a fleshy-leaved plant, flowers yellow, summer southern Europe.

Cultivation The half-hardy annual species are grown from seeds sown in an ordinary seed compost at a tem-perature of 60°F (16°C) and the seed-lings pricked off when they are large enough to handle into small pots. Finally they are planted out on rock gardens or in sunny borders in well-drained soil. When grown in the green-house in pots, they are placed in very sandy soil and kept in a sunny position, being watered freely in late spring and summer. The temperature in summer should be between 65–70°F (18–21°C), and in winter about 50°F (10°C). Propa-gation is by seed, as for most succulents, covered very lightly or not at all, or from cuttings, rooted in sandy soil at any time.

Top left: for the collector, a greenhouse devoted to cacti and other succulents can be an absorbing hobby.
Top right: One of the crassulas, Crassula arborescens.
Centre right: Sempervivum tecotrum calcareum.
Above: Echinopsis obrepanda, a Bolivian cactus.
Above far left: One of the succulent Portulacas. This one shows the congested growth of Portulaca pygmea, with fleshy leaves.
Above left: Foquieria splendens, a xerophyte growing in Arizona under very dry conditions.

Tropical plants for greenhouse or home

Plants are very adaptable and although greenhouse plants come from a wide range of climates, soils, temperature and rainfall, most tolerate the conditions we can provide at home or in a greenhouse, if a few simple facts are noted.

Choice

Important considerations before selecting a plant, are the place it will occupy, the conditions in which it will live and why it will be grown. Some plants require hot, dry, sunny sites while others prefer cool, moist, shady places and yet others need differing conditions during a resting period. Many are grown for the beauty of their flowers alone, but this is usually restricted to a short time in the year so foliage is an asset, unless there is an alternative place to keep the plant during the flowerless periods. There are plenty of species grown specially for the different shape, colour and texture of their leaves or even because the plant is bushy, trailing or climbing. When buying it is advisable to check that a plant is free from the pests often found on the lower leaf surfaces and around the growing tips and that it is generally healthy. At home, it is best to treat the plant gently for a week without excessive heat, light or water.

Care

The five major factors for the care of plants are light, water, heat, air and food.

Light Without enough light a plant cannot live and will become straggly, with small pale leaves and few flowers. Plants will grow towards a unilateral light source so that regularly turning the pot slightly may prevent uneven growth. Flowering or variegated-leaved plants need brighter light than foliage plants but in summer shading is often necessary.

Water Each plant has unique water requirements and the faster it grows the more it needs. In winter, watering should be reduced but in spring as the new growth begins, more can be given and plants in small pots will require relatively more. However, overwatering is as harmful as underwatering as it may cause rotting of the crown or prevent the roots from breathing. Rain water is ideal especially for species requiring a lime-free soil, unless it is polluted or stagnant. Plants should not be watered in bright sunlight to avoid scorching splashed leaves.

Heat A steady temperature without draughts is more important than high heat. Most species will grow well at temperatures below those of their natural habitats but the minimum temperature is an important consideration in choosing plants for certain places. Some plants prefer a lower temperature during resting periods.

Air Fresh air is essential and gas, oil or coke fumes without adequate ventilation can kill sensitive species. Some types of heating, especially central heating, can also dry the air. Humidity is just as important as air and can be achieved in several ways. Humidifiers will moisten the whole area or individual pots can be put in a larger container of moist peat or moss, the pots may be stood on pebbles in a dish filled with water or the leaves may be syringed with water—as long as this is not done in full sun.

Food A green plant can produce all the food it needs using light, air, water and the minerals found in the soil. In a reputable brand of potting compost these minerals should not initially be in short supply. However, a pot contains a limited amount of medium so that the available nutrients are depleted more quickly than if the plant roots are in the ground. Liquid fertilizers ensure even distribution of mineral salts to the roots of potted plants and are usually applied when watering during the growing or flowering seasons, but not during resting periods. Nitrates are essential for general growth and leaf development, phosphates for good root formation and potash for flower production. Several 'trace' elements are required in lower concentrations and are less likely to be in short supply in the soil.

General maintenance

When a plant becomes pot-bound, that is, too large for its container, the roots begin to grow through the drainage hole at the base, the soil needs frequent watering, the growth rate slows and when removed from the pot, a mass of roots can be seen with little apparent soil. Repotting is best done towards the beginning of the growing season. A clean, slightly larger pot should be chosen, the drainage hole covered with crocks, then a layer of compost. The plant is knocked out of the old pot by gently tapping the inverted pot on a hard surface while supporting the plant with the other hand. The old crocks are removed, the roots teased out and any dead ones cut away. It is then placed in the centre of the new pot and the space filled with fresh damp compost, firmed down and well watered. While the roots become re-established, it is advisable to keep the plant out of the full sun.

To retain a good appearance and avoid pests or disease, dead or discoloured flowers and leaves should be removed and, unless the foliage is very hairy, an occasional syringe with water helps to remove any dust or soot which can clog the stomata or breathing pores. Climbing plants require training by carefully tying the young growth before it becomes too brittle on to a suitable framework of canes and wire. Some plants may need staking but trailing plants are best if allowed to fall naturally and a hanging basket is ideal. To prevent untidy growth, and improve the shape of a plant some of the growing tips may be pinched out just above a leaf bud to encourage branching and bushiness.

Propagation

Raising plants from seed is fascinating but many require a higher temperature for germination than is needed for growth, and it often takes a long time for the plant to reach flowering size. The seeds are sown in a seed compost and once the seedlings have appeared they must be kept moist. They should be pricked out into potting compost in a larger container before becoming crowded to avoid weak, spindly plants. Other plants may be increased by dividing the roots or by offsets, the small plants growing from the base of the parent plant which can be cut away and potted up. Cuttings are another means of increase but the type of cutting will depend on the plant involved. These require a moist, well drained compost such as a mixture of peat and sand and a warm, humid atmosphere ventilated daily to prevent moulds.

Pests and disease

A healthy, well cared-for plant should not succumb to pests or disease, especially if new ones are carefully examined or even quarantined before they come into contact with existing plants. The troubles that might occur if the basic rules are ignored are root rot, mildew due to excessive water or humidity, white-fly, aphids and red spider mites which can be controlled by chemical pesticides or by destroying infected plants.

Flowering plants

Clivia

Named in honour of a Duchess of Northumberland, a member of the Clive family (*Amaryllidaceae*). Kafir Lily. A small genus of bulbous plant from South Africa, with evergreen leaves and showy flowers. All have strap-shaped glossy leaves, 1–2 feet long. They are occasionally referred to as Imantophyllums.

Species cultivated *C. × cyrtanthiflora*, orange flowers, winter to spring, hybrid. *C. gardenii*, orange-yellow flowers, December to February. *C. × kewensis*, canary-yellow, spring, hybrid. *C. miniata*, usually scarlet and yellow, but variable, spring, the most popular species from which many varieties and hybrids have been raised in different colours. *C. nobilis*, red and yellow, May to July.

Cultivation Clivias need a temperature of between 50–60°F (10–16°C) in spring and summer and should be watered freely and syringed frequently during this period. In winter they should be kept cool 45–50°F (7–10°C) and given little water, as this is the resting period. Pot plants in February in a compost of 2 parts of loam, 1 part of decayed manure and sand, or in loam plus leafmould and a little bonemeal and charcoal, if decayed manure is not available. They should be given a sunny position in the greenhouse, close to the glass. Propagation is by seed sown in March in a propagating case at a temperature of 75°F (24°C), or by divison at potting time, which is possible but not easy. Offshoots should be carefully removed and potted up.

Columnea

In honour of an Italian nobleman, Fabius Columna, author of the earliest botanical book illustrated with copper plates, published in Naples in 1592 (*Gesneriaceae*). Evergreen trailing sub-shrubs for stove or warm greenhouses, principally from Mexico and Costa Rica. They are particularly suited for culture in hanging baskets, which gives the long growth a chance to develop fully and the bold, tubular blossoms to be displayed properly.

Species cultivated *C. banksii*, scarlet flowers, early summer. *C. gloriosa*, scarlet and yellow flowers, summer; var. *purpurescens*, purple foliage, scarlet and yellow flowers, summer. *C. magnifica*, scarlet flowers, early summer. *C. microphylla*, scarlet and yellow flowers, summer. *C. schiedeana*, scarlet flowers, summer.

Cultivation Columneas require an open

Top: Clivia miniata, a bulbous plant with evergreen foliage, introduced from Natal.
Right: Columnea gloriosa, a pendulous growing epiphyte. The form here, purpurea, has bronze-coloured foliage.

and well-drained compost with few added nutrients. Temperatures: 65–70°F (18–21°C) spring to autumn, 60°F (16°C), (55°F (13°C) positive minimum) from autumn through to spring. Water freely and maintain humid conditions during the warm season, much less so during the cool, darker months. Propagation is by cuttings of shoots taken in the latter half of April and rooted in a warm frame at 65°F (18°C) with bottom heat. Repot at the end of March.

Euphorbia

There are many greenhous species cultivated as well as succulents including the well known Poinsettia.

Greenhouse species cultivated *E. fulgens* (syn. *E. jacquinaeflora*), 2–3 feet, small leafy shrub, scarlet bracts carried on the upper side of young shoots, autumn and winter, Mexico. *E. pulcherrima* (syn. *Poinsettia pulcherrima*), poinsettia, 3–6 feet, brilliant scarlet showy bracts in winter, Mexico. The modern Ecke hybrids are increasing in popularity. They include 'Barbara Ecke', fluorescent carmine bracts; 'Pink Ecke', coral pink and 'White Ecke', white. Some have variegated foliage. Even more popular now is the Mikkelsen strain, introduced in 1964. These, with shorter stems and with bracts in scarlet, pink or white, are a good deal 'hardier' in that they will withstand lower temperatures and fluctuating temperatures, yet will retain their bracts and remain colourful for 5–6 weeks.

Cultivation A good compost is 4 parts of fibrous loam, 1 part of decayed cow manure and a half part of silver sand. Young plants should be potted into 6- or 8-inch pots in summer and kept in a cold house or frame until September. Then feed regularly with a liquid feed and bring into a temperature of 60–65°F (16–18°C) to bring the plants into flower in December. After flowering, reduce watering and temperature until the soil is quite dry. In April cut back to two buds and start to water. Repot in May when the young shoots are about 1 inch long. Pot on as required; in high summer the pots can be stood out of doors or kept in a cold frame and brought in again in September. Propagation is from cuttings of young shoots taken in summer and inserted in sand in a temperature of 70°F (21°C).

Exacum

From the Latin *ex*, out of, *ago*, to drive; the plant was thought to expel poison (*Gentianaceae*). Greenhouse an-

Top: Euphorbia pulcherrima, the Poinsettia, has flamboyant bracts. 'Mikkelsen Pink' is an example of a newer strain.
Right: Exacum affine has fragrant bluish-lilac flowers, with prominent golden stamens. It is an attractive pot plant.

nuals, biennials and perennials first grown in the west in the middle of the 19th century for their freely produced flowers.

Species cultivated *E. affine*, 6 inches, fragrant, bluish-lilac flowers, June to October, Socotra; var. *atrocaeruleum*, gentian-blue. *E. macranthum*, 1½ feet, purple, summer, Sri Lanka. *E. zeylanicum*, 2 feet, violet-purple, summer, Sri Lanka.

Cultivation Exacums like a compost of equal parts of loam, peat, sand and leafmould and need a minimum winter temperature of 50°F (10°C). Sharp drainage is essential as the plants are particularly liable to damp off. The atmosphere should be moist and shade is needed from hot sun. Propagation is from seed, sown in August and September, the seedlings over-wintered in small pots and potted on into 5 inch pots in March for summer flowering.

Episcia

From the Greek *episkios*, shaded, a reference to the natural habitat of the plants (*Gesneriaceae*). Natives of tropical America, these herbaceous perennials are grown as decorative foliage and flowering plants in a warm greenhouse.

Species cultivated *E. chontalensis*, 6 inches, trailing, flowers white or pale lilac with yellow centre, autumn and winter. *E. cupreata*, 6 inches, trailing, flowers scarlet, leaves with red and silver bands. *E. fulgida*, 6 inches, trailing, scarlet, July.

Cultivation The episcias are admirable plants for hanging baskets or in large pans on raised staging. Pot or plant in March or April in a compost of equal parts of fibrous peat, peat and leafmould, with some sharp sand added. They require a shady position and a winter temperature of about 60°F (16°C), rising to 65–80°F (18–27°C) from March to September. Propagation is by cuttings inserted in sandy peat in March or April with a temperature of about 80°F (27°C).

Gesneria

In honour of Conrad Gesner, sixteenth-century Swiss botanist (*Gesneriaceae*). Tuberous rooted perennials for the warm greenhouse, mostly natives of Brazil. The foliage of many is ornamental, often velvety in appearance and the long-tubed flowers are borne in spikes.

Species cultivated *G. cardinalis* (syn. *G. macrantha*), 15 inches, scarlet flowers, autumn; var. *compacta*, 1 foot. *G. donkelaeriana*, 1–2 feet, leaves tinged with red and purple, vermilion flowers, summer. *G.* × *exoniensis*, 1 foot, leaves velvety with red hairs, orange, scarlet and yellow flowers, winter, hybrid. *G.* × *refulgens*, 1½ feet, violet and white flowers, summer, hybrid. There are also new hybrids available in combinations of white, yellow, orange and pink, ranging from 1–1½ feet in height.

Cultivation Pot up the tubers between March and June to extend the season of

Above: Episcias cupreata and lilacina, natives of tropical America, require a warm greenhouse when grown for ornamental foliage and flowers. Right: An orange-flowered hybrid Gesneria, a genus of plants mainly from Brazil.

flowering, in a well-drained compost of 2 parts of fibrous peat, 1 part of good loam, 1 part of leafmould, sand and decayed manure. An even temperature, between 55°F (13°C) in the winter and 70°F (21°C), plus sun heat in the summer is ideal. Water freely before flowering, gradually decreasing afterwards. Propagation is from leaf cuttings in spring and summer in a temperature of 70–75°F (21–24°C) or from seed sown in January on the surface of fine compost in a temperature of not less than 55°F (13°C).

Gloxinia

Commemorating Benjamin Peter Gloxin, eighteenth-century physician and botanist, of Colmar (*Gesneriaceae*). Hot house tuberous rooted plants with elaborately coloured velvety flowers and hairy leaves, frequently flushed red. The gloxinias have all been developed from *Sinningia speciosa* (syn. *Gloxinia speciosa*) a Brazilian plant with violet flowers. Varieties all produce trumpet-shaped flowers with a wide mouth, scalloped and characterised by a glorious range of colour. Some are self-colours, most are spotted or edged with other colours.

Such named varieties as 'Beacon',

crimson; 'Blanche de Meru', pale pink, edged white; 'Cyclops', rose-red and white; 'Defiance', bright scarlet; 'Emperor Frederick', red, edged white; 'Emperor William', blue, edged white; 'Giant Purple'; 'Giant White'; 'Grenadier', intense scarlet; 'Mont Blanc', pure white; 'Mauve Queen'; 'Pink Beauty', soft pink; 'Prince Albert', violet-blue; 'Princess Elizabeth', light blue with white throat; and 'Roi des Rouges' ('Waterloo'), dark red, are obtainable and, in addition, seedsmen offer selections under such names as 'Invincible Prize Superb Mixed', 'Spotted Hybrids', 'Heatherset Hybrids', etc. All grow 9–12 inches tall.

Cultivation The tubers should be started into growth in succession between January and April in a temperature of 60–65°F (16–18°C). Pot up when there is about 3 inches of growth, shading, watering liberally and potting on as required through the early summer. A suitable compost consists of equal proportions of loam, fibrous peat, leaf-mould, well-rotted manure and a scattering of silver sand.

Reduce the temperature to about 55°F (13°C) once the flower buds form, when weak liquid feeds are helpful. After flowering gradually reduce the watering, dry off and rest the tubers. Propagation is from seed sown in a temperature of 70°F (21°C) (preferably with bottom heat) in January or February. Maintain a moist atmosphere, prick off and pot up, when the temperature can be reduced to 60–65°F (16–18°C). Damp down the house regularly, but do not let the leaves get wet as they are liable to rot. To propagate a choice variety leaf cuttings may be taken at any time, and inserted in sand in a propagating case. The chief pest is thrips which cause much damage to leaves and flower stalks but well-grown tubers should last and flower for several years.

Haemanthus
From the Greek *haima*, blood, and *anthos*, flower, alluding to the deep red flower colour of some species (*Amaryllidaceae*). Blood lily. Greenhouse bulbous plants, natives of tropical and South Africa, usually with long, broad leaves and showy flowers, many in a dense head, the stamens often protuding.

Species cultivated *H. albiflos*, 1 foot, flowers white or greenish-white with protruding stamens, June. *H. coccineus*, 9 inches, large fluffy heads of coral-red flowers with red bracts, September; the leaves lie flat and develop after the flowers and die off in the following summer. *H. katherinae*, 1–2 feet, flowers scarlet on separate stalks, July; leaves do not die away at the time of flowering. *H. magnificus*, 15 inches, large head of orange-scarlet flowers with golden stamens, July; leaves on a separate stem; needs stove conditions. *H. natalensis*, 2 feet, green, orange and purple flowers, February. *H. puniceus*, 1 foot, scarlet with yellow or orange stamens, summer.

Cultivation Pot the early-flowering kinds in autumn and the later-flowering ones in spring, placing the bulbs to half their

Top: Gloxinias are plants for the warm greenhouse, and have velvety flowers. Above: The large, showy flowers of Haemanthus katharinae.

depth on a compost of 2 parts by volume of sandy loam, 1 part of each of peat, sand and decayed manure. Water very little until growth begins, then only moderately, withholding water altogether after flowering. Plants require a temperature ranging from 45°F (7°C) in winter to 65°F (18°C) in summer, or up to 55°F (13°C) as a minimum winter temperature for *H. coccineus*. The best results are obtained from bulbs not disturbed more than every fourth year. Propagation is from offsets at potting time.

Hedychium
From the Greek *hedys*, sweet, *chios*, snow; some species have white, fragrant flowers (*Zingiberaceae*). Butterfly lily, ginger lily. A genus of greenhouse evergreen perennials with rhizomatous rootstocks, from South and East Asia, and Malagasy, grown for their fragrant flowers.

Species cultivated *H. coronarium*, fragrant garland flower, 3–5 feet, white flowers, summer, India. *H. gardnerianum*, 4 feet, lemon-yellow flowers, summer, Himalaya.

Cultivation *H. gardnerianum* may be grown in a cool greenhouse but *H. coronarium* should have a winter temperature of 50–55°F (10–13°C). Pot in March or April, or plant in a greenhouse border or in large tubs which can be placed out of doors in summer. The compost should consist of 1 part of sandy loam and 2 parts of leafmould. Give the plants plenty of water from April to November, less in winter. Cut down the flower stems immediately after flowering. Propagate by division of the rhizomes in March or April.

Hibiscus
An ancient Greek name given to a mallow-like plant (*Malvaceae*). Rose mallow. A genus comprising species, most of which are greenhouse perennial plants in the temperate zones, though one popular species is a hardy deciduous shrub. There are also hibiscus which, in their natural environment, produce tropical fruits. These can be grown as flowering annuals. They are mostly natives of the tropics.

Greenhouse species cultivated *H.* × *archeri* (*H. schizopetalus* × *H. rosa-sinensis*), 6–8 feet, flowers red, summer, similar to those of the latter parent, hybrid. *H. cameronii*, 2 feet, rose-coloured flowers, July, Malagasy. *H. coccineus*, 6 feet, scarlet flowers, July and August, South N. America. *H. manihot*, to 10 feet, large flowers, 6 inches across, yellow with maroon centre, late summer, China, Japan. *H. rosa-sinensis*, blacking plant, 8 feet, showy crimson flowers, 4–5 inches across, summer, Asia. Many named varieties of this species have been raised, with single, semi- and fully-double flowers in various shades. *H. schizopetalus*, 10 feet, brilliant orange-red pendulous flowers, summer, east tropical Africa.

Cultivation Greenhouse species are usually trained to a support from pots or borders containing a well-drained compost. Prune as required, in February. Water freely during summer, less in winter. Summer temperature can go up to 75°F (24°C), with a winter minimum of 55°F (13°C). *H. manihot* can be grown from seed annually for flowering as a tender pot plant. All are propagated by seeds sown in a temperature of 75°F (24°C) in March, or by cuttings of near-ripe shoots rooted in a close frame, in a temperature of 75°F (24°C) in spring or summer.

Hippeastrum

Derived from the Greek *hippeus*, a knight, *astron*, a star, possibly in connection with a resemblance to knights and stars as seen in *H. equestre* (*Amaryllidaceae*). A genus of S. American, greenhouse, bulbous plants often referred to as *Amaryllis*, to which they are closely related. The large, showy, trumpet flowers of the hybrids, ranging in colour from the richest velvety crimson to the more delicate shades of pink and white, also bicolored, rank them among the most prized of winter and spring flowering pot plants for the greenhouse. Most of the hippeastrums offered in trade lists are of hybrid origin.

Species cultivated *H. aulicum*, 2 feet, crimson and purple flowers, winter. *H. pardinum*, 2 feet, flowers green, yellow and scarlet, spring. *H. pratense*, 2 feet, scarlet flowers, spring and early summer. *H. procerum*, 3 feet, bluish-mauve flowers, spring. *H. psittacinum*, 2 feet, flowers orange and scarlet, summer. *H. puniceum* (syn. *H. equestre*), Barbados lily, 18 inches, red flowers, summer. *H. reginae*, 2 feet, red and white flowers, spring. *H. reticulatum*, 1 foot, flowers rose or scarlet, spring. *H. rutilum*, 1 foot, crimson and green flowers, spring. *H. vittatum*, 2 feet, flowers crimson and white, spring. Cultivars include 'Fire Dance', vermilion; 'Picotee', pure white, petals edged red; 'Queen of the Whites', faintly grey inside; 'Rilona', pure salmon; 'Wyndham Hayward', dark red, deeper inside.

Cultivation Pot new bulbs in January, choosing a pot size to leave no more than ¾ inch width of soil between the bulb and the pot rim. Bulbs should be planted to half their depth only, in an average compost, or a mixture of 2 parts of turfy loam, and 1 part of sharp sand, plus a double handful of bonemeal to each bushel of the mixture. Start them into growth in a temperature of 60°F (16°C) and give no water for the first two weeks,

Top: A form of Hibiscus rosa-sinensis, with showy flowers in summer.
Right: Hippeastrum evansii, a charming yellow and white species.

then start with small amounts. As flower spikes appear, within about 3 weeks of being started, the temperature can rise to 65–70°F (18–21°C) by day, with a night minimum of 60°F (16°C). Keep the plants well watered and fed with liquid manure while growing, syringeing twice daily and maintaining a humid atmosphere. Remove dead flower heads if seed is not required. Gradually reduce the water supply from July to September (according to the time the bulbs were started into growth) until the pots are stored dry in a minimum temperature of 40°F (4°C) for winter. Examine and repot as necessary in January, removing all dead roots. Renew the surface compost of bulbs not repotted, and start them into growth.

Young plants raised from seed should not be dried off for the winter until after their first flowering, but will need less water while the older bulbs are resting. Sow seed as soon as it is ripe, in a temperature of 60–65°F (16–18°C). Grow on in quantities in large pots or boxes until plants are about 6 inches tall, then pot them individually into 4-inch pots for their first flowering. Named or selected forms are increased by offsets removed and potted separately when the plants are inspected in January.

Hymenocallis

From the Greek *hymen*, a membrane, *kallos*, beauty, referring to the cup-like membrane which unites the stamens (*Amaryllidaceae*). A genus of bulbous plants, for the warm greenhouse or stovehouse, containing both evergreen and deciduous species, all but one (which is a native of Guinea) coming mainly from South America. They are grown for their large, usually white, fragrant flowers, borne in clusters at the ends of long stalks. They are closely related to the genus *Ismene* and also *Pancratium*.

Species cultivated *H. calathina*, leaves narrow, 1 foot long, flowers white, very fragrant, several on a stem opening in succession, spring, Peru, greenhouse. *H. crassifolia*, leaves to 2 feet long, 2 inches wide, flowers white, borne in a cluster of four on a 2-foot tall stem, summer, Kentucky. *H. eucharidifolia*, leaves to 1 foot long, flowers white, funnel-shaped, with green tube, 4 or 5 in a cluster, on a 1 foot tall stem, spring, tropical America, stovehouse. *H. macrostephana*, leaves strap-shaped, to 3 feet long, flowers white, tube green, up to 8 flowers on a stem, South America, stovehouse. *H. ovata*, leaves strap-shaped, to 10 inches long, flowers white, fragrant, tube greenish, on a stem to 1 foot tall, autumn, West Indies, stovehouse. *H. speciosa*, leaves narrow to 2 feet long, to 4 inches wide, flowers white, very fragrant, on stems to 1 foot tall, West Indies, stovehouse.

Cultivation All species will succeed in a compost consisting of 2 parts of sandy

*Top: A scented plant for the greenhouse is Hymenocallis macrostephana, with several flowers carried on each stem.
Above: The scarlet flowers of the Brazilian Jacobinia coccinea appear in February.*

loam, 1 part of well-rotted manure and ½ a part of sharp sand. Pot in March every three or four years and keep the pots in a sunny part of the greenhouse. Plants will need ample water from April to September, less from September to December and should be kept quite dry from December to April. Once plants have started into growth, in May, they may be fed once or twice a week with weak liquid manure. *H. crassifolia* may be grown on the edges of indoor pools. Stove species require a minimum winter temperature of 55–65°F (13–18°C), ranging up to 80°F (27°C) in summer; greenhouse species should have a winter minimum of 45–50°F (7–10°C), rising in summer to 65°F (18°C). Propagation of all kinds is by offsets detached at potting time and potted up as recommended above. In mild areas *H. calathina* may be grown out of doors in a sheltered position, although the bulbs should still be lifted and stored in dry sand during the winter months. Plants may be attacked by mealy bug: control it with nicotine washes.

Jacobinia

From Jacobina, in South America, near Bahia. A genus of some 40 species of showy herbs and shrubs, from the hotter parts of America, introduced in Europe in the mid-eighteenth century (*Acanthaceae*). Stove flowering plants of easy cultivation, but which become weedy unless correctly pruned and cared for.

Species cultivated *J. carnea*, flesh pink, 3–4 feet, August–September. *J. chrysostephana*, 3 feet, yellow, winter. *J. ghiesbreghtiana* (syn. *Justicia ghiesbreghtiana*), 1½–2 feet, scarlet, December. *J. pauciflora* (syn. *Libonia pauciflora*), 2 feet, scarlet tipped yellow, winter. *J. suberecta*, 1 foot, bright scarlet, summer, low, spreading habit and excellent for a hanging basket in the warm house.

Cultivation Pot in March–April in equal parts by volume of loam, leafmould, peat and sand. Stand in a well lit stovehouse from September–June with a temperature of 55–65°F (13–18°C). Water moderately September–March, freely at other times. Pinch tips of young shoots between May–August, to encourage bushy growth. Stand in sunny frames, June–September, and apply liquid fertilizer twice a week to plants in flower. Prune shoots to within 1 inch of the base after flowering. Propagate by cuttings of young shoots placed in sandy soil under a hand light in a temperature of 75°F (24°C) between March and July.

Lachenalia

The name commemorates M. de la Chenal, professor of botany at Basel, 1736–1800 (*Liliaceae*). Greenhouse bulbous plants, natives of South Africa, with yellow or orange-red, drooping, tubular flowers on small spikes. These plants have been undeservedly neglected; they are very easy to manage and require slight heat only, and produce their flowers in winter or very early spring when they are most welcome.

Species cultivated *L. aloides nelsonii*, 1 foot, yellow, tinged green, spring. *L. bulbifera*, 9 inches, coral, tinged with green and purple, late spring.

Cultivation Pot up the bulbs, placing five or so in a 5-inch pot in September, and keep cool in a frame for at least two months. Use a compost with few added nutrients. As soon as sufficient roots have formed, take the pots into a slightly heated greenhouse and place them in a sunny position. After flowering, reduce water and allow the bulbs to dry out completely before repotting the following autumn. Propagate by seed sown in March, or small bulbs may be potted up in the autumn.

Lantana

The foliage of the lantana is similar to

Top: Lantana camara, from Jamaica, used for bedding or grown in the greenhouse.
Right: Lachenalia pendula.

that of the viburnum, *Lantana* being the old name for the latter *(Verbenaceae)*. These shrubs are grown in the greenhouse in the British Isles, and are mostly natives of the warmer parts of North America. They can be planted out in the early summer in sandy soil in a sunny bed or border and then lifted and taken into the greenhouse again and repotted in September. The flower heads are very like those of verbena—the colours range from white to violets, oranges and reds.

Species cultivated *L. camara*, 4 feet, pink or yellow, becoming red or orange, June, Jamaica. *L. chelsonii*, 2 feet, orange-red, summer, South America. *L. montevidensis* (syn. *L. selloviana*), rose-lilac, winter and summer, Montevideo. *L. nivea* (syn. *L. camara nivea*), 2 feet, white, late summer, East Indies.

Cultivation Sandy but rich compost is best, so use ordinary branded potting composts or a mixture of loam, peat, leafmould or manure, and sand. Pot in the spring and place the pots in a sunny position in the greenhouse and water well during the summer. The temperature should be 65°F (18°C) in the summer and 55°F (13°C) in the winter months. Feed well in the summer with liquid manure. In their natural habitat these shrubs thrive in the hot, dry conditions of the tropical climates and make large, sprawling shrubs; to keep them within bounds in the greenhouse they should be pruned in February. Propagate by seeds sown in a sandy mixture containing peat and leafmould in spring. Keep the temperature at about 75°F (24°C). Propagate also from cuttings taken either in spring or late summer; insert in a sandy mixture in a closed propagating frame in a temperature of 65°F (18°C). If striking cuttings in the spring, raise the temperature slightly.

Medinilla

Commemorating J. de Medinilla of Pineda, Spanish Governor of the Marianne Islands, in 1820 *(Melastomataceae)*. This genus of 150 tropical shrubs some of them climbers, has several species which are cultivated in the stovehouse or warm greenhouse. They have showy flowers, and sometimes, in addition, coloured bracts and good foliage. A humid atmosphere is needed.

Species cultivated *M. curtisii*, 3 feet, ivory white with purple anthers, spring, Sumatra. *M. javanensis*, 3 feet, pale rose, purple anthers, leaves tinged red beneath, winter, Java. *M. magnifica*, 3 feet, rose-pink, pink bracts, summer, Philippines; this and its variety *superba* are the most strikingly beautiful of these shrubs. *M. teysmanni*, 4 feet, rose-pink, spring, Celebes, New Guinea.

Cultivation A good loam with added charcoal is needed. Pot firmly to encourage short, firm growth, and pot on frequently as the roots increase rapidly. Water and syringe freely during the growing season, but moderately only

Above left: The flowers of Medinilla magnifica are enhanced by wide pink bracts.
Right: The pale pink flowers of Nerium oleander are carried in terminal clusters in summer.

during the winter. The atmosphere must be kept drier during the flowering period. Propagation is by cuttings of half-ripe shoots placed in a propagating case in a temperature of 70°F (21°C).

Nerium

An ancient Greek name for this plant, possibly from *neros*, humid, referring to its natural waterside habitat *(Apocynaceae)*. Oleander, rose bay. A genus of 2 or 3 species of tender evergreen shrubs of great merit as greenhouse specimens on account of their magnificent large clusters of flowers, mostly pink, borne in early summer. *N. oleander* has provided the majority of forms in cultivation. Neriums are extremely poisonous plants and have caused the deaths of animals and people who have eaten flowers or foliage.

Species cultivated *N. odorum*, 6–8 feet, fragrant flowers, pale to dark pink, in terminal cymes, summer, northern India to Japan; var. *flore-pleno*, double flowers, rose pink. *N. oleander*, 6–10 feet, flowers in terminal cymes, deep pink, summer. Cultivars: forms are listed in catalogues mostly by their colours, e.g. double white, double pink, double salmon pink, single red; also *variegata*, with yellow and green foliage.

Cultivation Pot up the shrubs in March, in large pots, tubs or other containers, in a compost of 2 parts of sandy loam,

1 part of leafmould, 1 part of well-rotted manure and 1 part of sand. They will need repotting in future years only when they become completely rootbound. Water the plants freely and sustain them by regular feeding throughout the summer. Syringe the foliage regularly to discourage red spider mite, a troublesome pest. Reduce the water supply from mid-September through the winter. Prune the plants when the flowers fade by cutting the new shoots hard back after which the plants should be kept on the dry side until new growth breaks. Propagation is by late summer cuttings of ripe wood, rooted in a soil-warmed propagating case. The cuttings should be 3–6 inches long and it is best to insert them singly in 2-inch pots, using a compost of sand, peat, leafmould and loam.

Plumbago

From the Latin *plumbum*, lead; one species was thought to be a remedy for lead poisoning, hence the name *(Plumbaginaceae)*. Leadwort. A genus of 12 species of shrubs, sub-shrubs, annual and perennial herbaceous plants, natives of the warmer parts of the world. The most commonly seen, *P. capensis*, makes a good climbing shrub for the greenhouse and may also be grown as a houseplant. The flowers are carried in spikes at the ends of the trailing stems and are very freely produced.

Greenhouse species cultivated *P. capensis*, Cape leadwort, climbing shrub, 10–15 feet, flowers powder blue, produced throughout late summer, South Africa; var. *alba*, white.

Stovehouse species cultivated *P. rosea*,

perennial, 2 feet, purplish-red flowers, July, East Indies. *P. zeylanica*, shrub, 18 inches, flowers white in long spikes, June, East Indies.

Cultivation Potting or planting should be carried out in the spring, using a compost of leafmould, peat and some sand and loam, or a brand of rich compost. Plant the climbing species in a greenhouse border where it can be trained against a wall, trellis or pillar. Large-sized pots or tubs can be used if no border is available, and it can also be used out of doors in the summer as a bedding plant. The stove species need a temperature of around 65°F (18°C) in the winter months, but *P. capensis* requires a temperature of about 45°F (7°C) only. Any frost-proof greenhouse, conservatory or living room is suitable. Water freely in the summer and feed with a liquid fertilizer, but keep the plants rather dry in the winter months. After flowering, prune back the flowered stems almost to their bases to encourage new growth in the spring which will bear next season's flowers. Propagation of the shrubs is best carried out in April by cuttings taken with a heel and inserted in a sandy compost in a propagating frame. Seeds may be sown in spring in a temperature of around 65°F (18°C).

Protea

From *Proteus*, the versatile sea-god, referring to the diversity of the species *(Proteaceae)*. In this genus there are some 130 species of evergreen shrubs, mostly natives of South Africa, but also some from tropical Africa. In the northern hemisphere these are plants for the greenhouse, although some species can be grown out of doors in sheltered, frost-free areas of Britain, Canada and the east coast areas of the United States. In nature they are subjected annually to a long dry season and strong sun, but unfortunately these conditions do not often occur in Britain. The leaves are tough and serrated and the flowers, which are produced at the ends of shoots, are borne in very large and showy dense heads, often being surrounded by series of brightly coloured bracts; the heads remain colourful over a long period. In appearance proteas are quite unlike any shrub which grows in temperate zones, though the flowers of some have been compared to the inflorescence of the globe artichoke *(Cynara scolymus)*, a resemblance which is commemorated in the names of two species described below, *P. cynaroides* and *P. scolymocephala*.

Species cultivated *P. compacta*, Bot River protea, to 10 feet, flowers clear pink in heads up to 4 inches across,

Top: The Cape Leadwort, Plumbago capensis, is a climbing shrub which produces powder blue flowers.
Right: Protea latifolia, the Ray-flowered Protea, is a South African plant.

Cape Province. *P. cordata*, 18 inches, flowers purple, flowerheads 2½ inches across, South Africa. *P. cynaroides*, king protea, to 6 feet, flowers white to pale pink, flowerheads to 8 inches or so across, spring and early summer. Cape Province. *P. grandiceps*, peach protea, to 5 feet, leaf margins sometimes red, flowers rosy-red and creamy-white, heads to 6 inches across, Cape Province. *P. grandiflora*, waboom, to 10 feet, flowers yellowish-green, bracts reddish-brown, flowerheads to 5 inches across, May and June, Cape Province. *P. lacticolor*, baby protea, to 6 feet, flowers pink and cream, in small heads, South Africa. *P. latifolia*, ray-flowered protea, to 8 feet, flowers pink, carmine or green, heads 5 inches across, June to August, Cape Province. *P. longiflora*, cream protea, to 6 feet, flowers cream or pink in heads to 6 inches long, Cape Province. *P. longifolia*, long-leaved protea, to 6 feet, leaves large and narrow, flowers white, black or purple tipped, bracts yellowish-green, heads to 4 inches across, February–April, South Africa. *P. mellifera*, honey-protea, true sugarbush, to 8 feet, flowers white, pink or red, heads to 3 inches across, September, Cape Province. *P. scolymocephala*, to 3 feet, flowers normally greenish-yellow, but variable in colour, heads to 5 inches across, May and June, South Africa. *P. suzannae*, suzanne protea, to 6 feet, flowers deep pink, heads 4–5 inches across, Cape Province. Other species and hybrids may be offered occasionally by specialist nurserymen and seedsmen.

Cultivation Proteas need the airiest and sunniest greenhouse treatment, and during June, July and August the pots must be put out of doors in a sunny sheltered spot. They dislike humid atmospheres. A very open soil mixture consisting of peaty loam and sharp sand, with a generous amount of charcoal and broken brick, is needed; drainage must be perfect. Potting on requires great care as the proteas resent root disturbance, and, as a regular measure the operation is not advisable as a pot-bound plant may flower more readily. The temperature in the winter should be between 40–50°F (4–10°C). Water moderately between March and September, and keep the soil just moist for the remainder of the time. Propagation is from imported seed or by cuttings of firm shoots taken in summer and inserted in well-drained pots of sand in a propagating frame with moderate bottom heat.

Rechsteineria

Commemorating Pfarrer Rechsteiner, a German botanist (*Gesneriaceae*). A genus with showy tubular flowers and tuberous roots, natives of South America. They were at one time part of the genus *Gesneria*, and are now in fact more correctly called by the generic name *Corytholoma*.

Species cultivated *R. cardinalis*, 12 inches, flowers velvety scarlet, July and August. *R. leucotricha*, 9–12 inches, silvery, intensely hairy leaves, flowers salmon or orange-red, summer. *R. lineata*, 1–2 feet, red, flowers purple-spotted, summer. *R. sellovia*, 4–5 feet, flowers pale red, summer. *R. warszewiczii*, maximum 2 feet, flowers orange-red, summer.

Cultivation These are plants for a greenhouse where the summer temperature is between 65–70°F (18–21°C). The winter temperature is less important, for the plants are then dormant, and should be about 50°F (10°C). Start the tubers into growth in March by placing them in boxes of sand and peat, but with the tops

Above: Rechsteineria cardinalis, a South American plant, has red flowers of a velvety texture.

of the tubers uncovered, in a temperature of 65–70°F (18–21°C). As roots develop, pot the plants singly into a compost of equal parts of leafmould, lime-free soil and coarse sand to which a little bonemeal is added. Pot very lightly making no attempt to firm the soil, but just tapping the pot so that the soil settles naturally. Water carefully at all times; the leaves, particularly those of *R. leucotricha*, are easily damaged by careless watering. Keep the house damped down at regular intervals and shade heavily. Do not allow the temperature to rise too high. After flowering, withhold water but do not allow the soil at any time to become dust dry. Keep it slightly moist so as to keep the tubers in good condition. Propagation can be carried out by seed sown thinly on to sterilized compost in January or February. Cuttings of shoots taken from the tubers, after they have been started into growth and the shoots have reached about 4 inches in height, will root if inserted in sand in a temperature of 70°F (21°C). New plants can also be raised from leaf cuttings.

Ruellia

Commemorating Jean de la Ruelle of Soissons, who wrote *De Natura Plantarum* in 1536 (*Acanthaceae*). A genus originally of some 200 species of annuals and perennials, but now reduced by botanists to 5 species. Most of the cultivated species are sub-shrubs with attractive flowers. They require greenhouse treatment.

Species cultivated *R. formosa*, a shrub, to 2 feet high, flowers scarlet in axillary cymes, each flower about 1½ inches long with two or three in each cyme, summer, Brazil. *R. macrantha*, sub-shrub to 3 feet, flowers purple-pink, 3½ inches long and 2 inches across, borne in the upper leaf axils, January–March, Brazil. *R. portellae*, prostrate herb rarely more than a few inches high, leaves purple on the undersides, flowers rosy, solitary, about 1½ inches long and 1 inch across, winter, Brazil.

Cultivation Branded potting composts are best used for these plants and the two winter-flowering species require a temperature of 55°F (13°C) during the winter, although if this falls to 50°F (10°C) during very cold spells no harm will be done. The lower temperature is quite sufficient for *R. formosa*. During the winter the plants will require plenty of light, but *R. portellae* will require shady conditions in the spring and summer. The other species will require very slight shade during the hottest months, but this should be only enough to prevent scorching. The winter-flowering species must be kept moist during their flowering period, but *R. macrantha* takes a decided rest during July and August and should be kept barely moist during this period. When flowering is completed, *R. formosa* and *R. macrantha* are cut hard back and the soil kept on the dry side until growth restarts. They are propagated by cuttings of young shoots, which should not be too soft. *R. portellae* can also be treated as an annual and propagated by seed.

Top: Ruellia macrantha, a winter-flowering species, has pink, open-mouthed flowers marked with maroon and yellow.
Right: The cultivars of Smithiana are available in a good colour range, and most have velvety leaves.

70

Smithiana

Named after Miss Matilda Smith, the botanical artist at Kew Gardens, London from 1887–1923 (*Gesneriaceae*). A genus of eight species of attractive flowering perennials with large, heart-shaped, velvety leaves, and spikes of orange, red or yellow tubular flowers. In recent years they have been much hybridised and there are many lovely varieties available. They are natives of Mexico. The generic name is sometimes spelt *Smithiantha*.

Species cultivated *S. cinnabarina*, 2 feet, flowers scarlet, summer. *S. multiflora*, 1½ feet, flowers white, August. *S. zebrina*, 2 feet, flowers yellow and scarlet, October. Cultivars include the following outstanding varieties: 'Abbey', peach and white; 'Alison', very pale to deeper pink; 'Carmell', flowers white, spotted red, leaves green, flushed red; 'Cathedral', flowers yellow-orange with pale spots; 'Dairy Maid', flowers golden yellow and salmon-orange, leaves dark green with purple and orange-red markings; 'Elke', flowers golden-orange and yellow, leaves olive-green and purple, with orange sheen; 'Firebird', flowers bright red and yellow, leaves olive-green, purple and orange; 'Moonlight', flowers primrose yellow, leaves olive green and purple; 'Orange King', flowers orange-yellow, leaves bronze; 'Pink Domino', flowers deep rose-pink and white; 'Rosemary', flowers carmine-rose and yellow, leaves violet-velvet; 'Santa Barbara', flowers carrot-red and pale yellow; 'Santa Clara', flowers salmon-orange to pink, leaves reddish; 'Sheila', flowers orange-pink, pink and yellow; 'Swan Lake', flowers creamy-white and salmon, leaves purple and green; 'Vespers', flowers orange with pale orange-red band.

Cultivation The compost should consist of peat, loam and leafmould in parts by volume of 2, 1 and 1, with a little silver sand and rotted organic material added. The tubers should be potted in February and March, with a minimum of covering, singly in 5-inch pots, and placed in a shaded part of the stovehouse; the pots should be well-drained, and the temperature 50–55°F (10–13°C). For flowering in summer potting should be carried out in March, in May for autumn flowering, and in June for winter-flowering. Water moderately until the young plants are 3 or 4 inches high, and then freely until growth begins to die down, and keep the soil dry while the plants are resting. Use a liquid fertilizer when the flower buds begin to show. The temperature from March to September should be 65–85°F (18–30°C), and for the remainder of the time 55–75°F (13–24°C). While the plants are resting the pots should be stored on

Right: The delicate flowers of Sparmannia africana, *the African Hemp which can mostly be grown only with greenhouse protection.*

their sides. Propagation is by seeds in spring, placed in a sand and peat compost in a temperature of 75–85°F (24–30°C), or by cuttings in spring in the same soil and temperature, or by dividing the tubers at potting time.

Sparmannia

Commemorating a Swedish traveller, Doctor Anders Sparmann (1748–1820), who accompanied Captain Cook on his second voyage of discovery (*Tiliaceae*). A genus of seven species of large evergreen shrubs or small trees with hairy leaves, natives of tropical Africa and South Africa and Malagasy.

Species cultivated *S. africana*, African hemp, to 20 feet or more, clusters of white flowers with a boss of prominent yellow and red or purple stamens; flowers are produced sporadically throughout the year. *S. palmata*, 10 feet, flowers white or purplish, with a prominent boss of yellow stamens, produced sporadically throughout the year.

Cultivation These plants can be grown out of doors in the mildest parts of the country. Elsewhere they require the protection of a temperate greenhouse where the minimum winter temperature is 45°F (7°C). They may be grown either in a well-drained sandy border,

or in pots in an ordinary soil such as a branded potting compost. They are fast-growing plants and need to be fed at regular intervals. A balanced fertilizer should be applied to the borders in spring before the new growth appears, and to pot plants at 3 or 4 weekly intervals during the growing season. Never overfeed, and ensure that the fertilizer mixture has the nitrogen balanced with the potash. Prune regularly, after the main flush of flowers, to keep the bushes compact. If this is neglected the bush becomes straggly. If space is limited, or where the plants are grown in pots, pruning may be necessary more than once a year. Grow the plants in full sun even in the height of summer. Water them frequently when they are in full growth but quite sparingly during the winter. Propagation is by cuttings of non-flowering shoots, which should be inserted into pure sand with bottom heat. These are generally easy to root but they can be temperamental, especially when hard or starved shoots are used for cutting material or when the shoots are soft.

Strelitzia

Named in honour of Queen Charlotte, the wife of George III, who was also Duchess of Mecklenburg-Strelitz (*Musaceae*). Bird of paradise flower. A genus of five species of large perennial herbaceous plants from southern Africa, grown for their large strikingly beautiful flowers.

Species cultivated *S. augusta*, a very large plant with leaf stems up to 6 feet long bearing an elliptic rounded leaf that may be 3 feet long. The inflorescence is composed of two spathes, shaped like a bird's head, from the middle of which emerge the white flowers, so that the plant suggests the head of a crested bird, spring. *S. reginae*, leaf stalk about 18 inches long, leaf-blade about the same length; the leaves radiate out in a fan; the flowers are orange and purple and very brilliant, emerging from the purplish spathes on a stem some 3 feet long. The plant is variable and among the varieties are the more compact, var. *humilis;* the attractive glaucous-leaved, var. *glauca;* and the more brilliant, var. *rutilans*, in which the leaves have a purple midrib, late spring.

Cultivation A rich potting compost suits these plants admirably. The winter temperature should not fall below 50°F (10°C) and during the summer high temperatures are relished. However, the plants resent a stuffy atmosphere and the ventilators should be opened whenever the temperature exceeds 65°F (18°C). During the summer the plants require abundant supplies of water and liquid feeding should be given at fortnightly intervals to established plants from the end of May until the beginning of September. The plants are kept on the dry side during the winter. Any potting on is best done about mid-March. During the summer the glass should be slightly shaded, but all possible light should be admitted from the end of September until late March or early April. Propagation is generally by detaching suckers and potting them up, but if the plants are hand-pollinated, seed will be set and will germinate in rather high temperatures. They take many years to arrive at flowering size. The plants are of relatively easy cultivation but take up a lot of room.

Zantedeschia

Commemorating Francesco Zantedeschi (1773–1846), Italian physician and botanist (*Araceae*). Arum or calla lily. A genus of eight or nine species of greenhouse rhizomatous perennials, natives of tropical Africa, grown for their handsome usually arrow-shaped leaves and arum-like flowers. *Z. aethiopica*, in particular, is much grown for the cut flower trade and is the 'arum lily' sold by florists.

Species cultivated *Z. aethiopica* (syn. *Richardia africana*), lily of the Nile, trumpet lily, 3–4 feet, flowers white, spathes to 10 inches long, winter and spring; varieties have been recorded with double or treble spathes. *Z. albomaculata*, 2 feet, leaves spotted white, flowers yellow or milk-white, summer. *Z. elliottiana*, 3 feet, flowers yellow, spathes 6 inches long, August. *Z. melanoleuca*, 18 inches, flowers yellow and purple, summer. *Z. rehmannii*, 2 feet, flowers rosy-purple, summer.

Cultivation For *Z. aethiopica* use a compost of equal parts of loam, cow manure and coarse silver sand. From October to May the plants should be in a greenhouse or indoors, but they can be either planted out of doors or the pots can be sunk up to their rims in moist, rich soil in summer. Repotting is needed annually in August or September. Moderate watering is required from September to March, but water freely from March to May. During the flowering period stimulants should be applied weekly. Out of doors water freely in dry weather. Temperatures should be 40–55°F (4–13°C) from September to March and 50–60°F (10–16°C) from March to May. Suitable stimulants are one teaspoonful of growth fertilizer; ½ ounce of guano; or ¼ ounce of nitrate of soda or sulphate of ammonia to 1 gallon of water. In mild areas *Z. aethiopica* may be grown in ponds, etc., provided the rhizomes are about 2½ feet below the surface to protect them from frost.

For the other species the compost is the same, but they should be grown in the greenhouse from October to June and in a cold frame for the rest of the year, repotting each year in February. Watering should be moderate from February to April and from August to October, and liberal from April to

August, but keep the soil nearly dry from October to February. Stimulants should be applied during the flowering period. Temperatures should be 55–65°F (13–18°C) from October to March, and 65–75°F (18–24°C) from March to October.

Propagation is by division when planting out of doors or repotting; by seeds sown ⅛ inch deep in loam, leaf-

Top: Strelitzia augusta, the Bird of Paradise, a plant for the warm greenhouse when grown in Britain. Above: Zantedeschia melancoleuca tropicanus has yellow flowers and spotted leaves.

mould and sand in a temperature of 65–75°F (18–24°C) in spring, or from suckers removed at potting time.

Flowers and foliage

Aechmea

From the Greek *aichme*, a point, refer-ring to the rigid points on the calyx (*Bromeliaceae*). Evergreens from tropi-cal America introduced in the early nineteenth century, long grown in stove-houses, but a few species are now grown successfully as house plants.

They are distinct from many plants because the leaves spring directly from the root, overlapping in rosette fashion to form a tube, through which the flower spike emerges. The flowers are short-lived but the colourful bracts may per-sist for many months.

Species cultivated *A. fulgens*, $1\frac{1}{2}$ feet, dark green leaves, purple flowers, per-sistent scarlet bracts; var. *discolor*, $2\frac{1}{2}$ feet, from Brazil, leaves maroon-purple below, greenish-grey above, purple-blue flowers, scarlet, persistent bracts. *A. mariae-reginae*, 2 feet, blue flowers, age-ing to pink, rose-pink bracts. *A. rhodo-cyanea* (*A. fasciata*), leaves 4 inches wide, 18 inches long, greyish-green band-ed with silver grey. Plants may be 2 feet or more across. The pink flower stem is $1\frac{1}{2}$ feet tall and bears lavender-blue flow-ers which last for a short time only, although the spiny pink bracts remain colourful for six months or more, before having to remove the dead rosette.

Cultivation The vase-like tube formed by the leaves should be kept filled with water, rainwater if available, preferably tepid in winter. In summer very dilute liquid fertilizer may be added occasion-ally. Watering of the compost should be reduced in winter, especially when the room temperature is low.

After flowering the rosette eventually dies but this may take six to twelve months during which time offsets will have formed which will themselves flow-er in due course. The dead rosette should be cut away cleanly with a sharp knife when it begins to look unsightly.

Propagation is by detaching the sucker-like offsets which arise at the side of the plant, in March, and potting them in sandy peat in a propagating case, then potting later into 6 inch pots. Compost: equal parts of fibrous loam, rough peat and leafmould. If possible maintain a winter temperature of 60–70°F (16–21°C), although *A. rhodocyanea* has proved to be surprisingly tough and will survive in much lower room temper-atures provided the compost is not kept wet.

Aphelandra

From the Greek *apheles*, simple, and *andros*, male, referring to the one-celled anthers (*Acanthaceae*). Evergreen shrubs from the tropics which must be grown in a greenhouse in the temperate zone, one is a popular house plant. The bracts surrounding the flowers over-lap one another giving the flower head a sculptured appearance.

Above: the lavender-blue flowers and persistent pink bracts of Aechmea rhodocyanea, a tough house plant.

Species cultivated *A. aurantiaca*, 3 feet, orange flower-heads. *A. pectinata*, 3 feet, scarlet. *A. squarrosal*, 3 feet, dark-green, ivory-banded leaves, yellow flow-er-heads, greenish-yellowish bracts; var. *louisae*, in which the leaves have ivory-white midribs and more distinctive ivory bands, is grown as a house plant. *A. tetragona*, 3 feet, scarlet.

Cultivation Grow these plants in pots in a moist atmosphere in a compost of peat, loam, leafmould and sand in equal parts. Summer temperature should be 70–80°F (21–27°C); slightly less in winter. Water freely in summer, sparingly in winter. Repot in March and prune in February, cutting the shoots to within 1 inch of their base. Propagate by cuttings rooted over bottom heat in a sandy compost in March or April. When grown in the house, *A. squarrosa louisae* does not need a high room temperature, 50°F (10°C) is adequate. It needs moderate watering in winter which should be in-creased when growth begins in the spring, when the plant should be repot-ted, using a rich potting compost. Potbound plants flower more readily; feeding should not begin until the flower buds appear.

Begonia

Commemorating Michel Bégon, 1638–1710, Governor of Canada, patron of botany (*Begoniaceae*). These half-hardy herbaceous and sub-shrubby plants are natives of moist tropical countries, apart from Australia. They need greenhouse treatment, though a large number are now used in summer bedding schemes.

The genus begonia is usually divided into two groups; those species with fibrous roots and those with tubers. Other classifications give special treatment to the winter-flowering forms, and to those grown exclusively for the interest of their leaves. A notable feature of begonias is their oblique, lop-sided or uneven sided leaves.

There has been so much hybridising in this genus that the naming has become quite complicated, and the custom of giving Latin specific names has not made matters easier.

The begonia, unlike the majority of plants, has, instead of hermaphrodite blooms, separate male and female blossoms on the same plant; the female flowers are generally removed as not being of much interest, though if seed is required, they must, of course, be retained. The seed is dust-fine and needs no covering of soil, in fact the raising of begonias from seed has something in common with the art of raising ferns from spores.

Species cultivated The best-known begonias are the hybrids of the tuberous species: *B. boliviensis*, *B. clarkei*, *B. einnabarina*, *B. davisii*, *B. pearcei*, *B. rosaeflora*, *B. veitchii*.

Another important group consists of the hybrids and varieties of *B. rex*, a plant from Assam with most interesting, colourful foliage. The winter-flowering and fibrous-rooted varieties derived from *B.* 'Gloire de Lorraine', a variety origin-

Left, above and below: These double-flowered begonias are two examples of large-flowered hybrids.
Right: 'Flamingo' is one of a number of Begonia semperflorens types often used for summer bedding.

ally raised in France in 1891 by the plant breeder Victor Lemoine, who crossed *B. socotrana* and *B. dregei*, form a most valuable group as they furnish the greenhouse at a difficult time of the year.

Fibrous-rooted species include: *B. acutifolia*, white, spring. *B. angularis*, white-veined leaves. *B. coccinea*, scarlet, winter. *B. evansiana*, pink, almost hardy (possibly hardy in the south-west). *B. fuchsioides*, scarlet, winter. *B. froebelli*, scarlet, winter. *B. foliosa*, white and rose, summer. *B. glaucophylla*, pink and pendulous, winter. *B. haageana*, pink, autumn. *B. hydrocotylifolia*, pink, summer. *B. incarnata*, rose, winter. *B. manicata*, pink, winter. *B. scharffiana*, white, winter. *B. semperflorens*, rose (has important large-flowered vars.). *B. socotrana*, pink, winter.

Nurserymen's catalogues contain long lists of hybrids of the above, too numerous to mention here, but in various shades of pink, red, cream and white with enormous double flowers in a number of different forms.

Species with ornamental leaves include: *B. albo-picta*, *B. argenteo-guttata*, white and pink speckled leaves. *B. hera-*

cleifolia, leaves deeply lobed. *B. imperialis*, velvety-green leaves. *B. boeringiana*, foliage purplish and green. *B. maculata*, foliage spotted white. *B. masoniana*, ('Iron Cross'), leaves green with a prominent dark 'iron cross' marking, popular as a houseplant. *B. metallica*, foliage has metallic lustre. *B. olbia*, bronze leaves spotted white. *B. rex*, foliage metallic silver and purple. *B. ricinifolia*, bronze leaves. *B. sanguinea*, leaves blood-red beneath. There are, in addition to the species given, many hybrids with beautiful leaves, especially named garden hybrids derived from *B. rex* and its varieties and other species, all known as Rex begonias.

Cultivation The fibrous-rooted begonias are usually obtained from seed, which should be sown in January in a temperature of 60°F (16°C). It is also possible to root growths from the base of the plant. The sub-shrubby perennial forms will come easily from normal cuttings, or all begonias may be raised by leaf cuttings. Leaf cuttings are single leaves which are pegged down in sandy compost, the undersides of all the main veins having been nicked with a razor blade. The temperature should be around 60–70°F (16–21°C). Little plants should form where veins were cut, and these may later be detached and potted-on separately. Most begonias need a winter temperature of about 60°F (16°C). The ornamental Rex type must not be ex-

74

posed to full sunlight, and many of the other classes will be happy with much less light than suits other greenhouse plants.

The tuberous begonias may, of course, be grown from tubers. These are usually started into growth by placing them in shallow boxes of peat or leafmould in February or March, hollow side uppermost, in a temperature of 60–70°F (16–21°C). After roots have formed the tubers are potted up in small pots and later moved into larger ones. A compost of equal parts of loam, leafmould, well-rotted manure and silver sand is suitable. Do not start to feed these tuberous plants till they have formed roots, or they will decay, but after they are rooted a bi-weekly dose of liquid manure is helpful. The tuberous begonias may also be raised from seed, and if this is sown in February plants may flower from July to October. These seed-raised plants are popular for summer bedding.

Tuberous begonias when their season is over must be gradually dried out. They may be left in their pots in a frost-proof shed, or knocked-out and stored in clean dry sand.

Gynura

From the Latin *gyne*, female, *oura*, tail, the stigma being long and rough (*Compositae*). A small genus of greenhouse perennials, native of tropical regions of India and Asia, grown for their ornamental foliage. The flower heads are solitary or in corymbs and are in varying shades of orange.

Species cultivated *G. aurantiaca*, 2–3 feet, stem and leaves covered with violet hairs which show especially on young plants, flowers brilliant orange in February. *G. sarmentosa*, a loosely twining plant, stems and foliage covered with dark purplish red hairs, flowers are orange and numerous. Frequently grown as a house plant.

Cultivation Pot plants in March in a compost of equal parts peat, loam, of leafmould and sand, and water freely throughout the summer and moderately after October. Maintain a winter temperature of 55–65°F (13–18°C). Propagation is by cuttings taken in March and April.

Neoregelia

Named after E. A. von Regel, a Russian botanist (*Bromeliaceae*). The genus was first named *Regelia*, and later *Aregelia*, two names still listed in some references and including, between them, the species mentioned below. There are about 40 species in the genus. The plants closely resemble other bromeliads such as aechmeas, with stiff, brightly-coloured leaves from a basal rosette which form a water-holding central 'vase'. Unlike those of aechmeas, the flowers of neoregelias are not carried on a spike but appear only just above the surface of the water in the 'vase'.

Species cultivated *N. carolinae tricolor*, leaves 12 to 15 inches, 1 inch wide, centrally striped yellow with pink tinge, central leaves carmine-red at flowering time, flowers purple-blue. *N. chantrieri* (syns. *Karatas × chantrieri*, *Nidularium × chantrieri*), leaves stiff, bright green, with dark mottling, tipped red, centre bright red, flowers white, hybrid. *N. marechali* (syn. *N. carolinae marechalii*), leaves flushed red when young, changing to green, inner leaves

Top: the leaves of Gynura sarmentosa are covered with purple-red hairs.
Above: Neoregelia meyendorfii has pink inner leaves at flowering time.

become carmine-red at flowering time, flowers lilac. *N. meyendorfii* (syn. *M. carolinae meyendorfii*), one of the smaller species with olive green leaves and central rosette of pink inner leaves at flowering time, lilac flowers. *N. spectabilis*, finger-nail plant, 12 inches, red tips to olive green leaves with metallic lustre, cross-banded grey beneath, blue flowers surrounded by central purple leaf rosette.

Cultivation These bromeliads do well in a compost of 2 parts of sphagnum moss, peat or leafmould, 1 part of fibrous loam, 1 part of coarse sand with a sprinkling of charcoal. Pots or containers must be well-drained. The central leaf 'vases' must be kept topped-up with water, preferably, rainwater. The minimum temperature should ideally be about 60°F (16°C) with atmospheric humidity, but plants will tolerate spells of cooler, drier conditions. These plants prefer less light than the majority of bromeliads. Propagation is by rooting larger offshoots, in a propagating case with bottom heat. Plants may be raised from seed but it takes a long time for plants to reach any size.

Climbing plants

Allamanda

Named after an eighteenth-century professor of natural history, Dr Fr. Allamand (*Apocynaceae*). Evergreen climbing plants from tropical America which need warm greenhouse conditions. Their large trumpet flowers make them among the most attractive of climbers.

Species cultivated *A. cathartica*, to 10 feet, has yellow flowers in June; vars. *grandiflora*, pale yellow flowers, 4½ inches across, *hendersonii*, yellow flowers, white-spotted in the throat, flushed brown outside, *nobilis*, bright yellow flowers with magnolia fragrance, *schotti*, large yellow flowers striped brown in the throat, *williamsii*, yellow flowers with reddish-brown throat, can be grown in bush form. *A. neriifolia*, erect-growing to 3 feet, with deep golden flowers streaked orange, June. *A. violacea*, 6–8 feet, large rosy-purple flowers in October. Does not do well unless grafted on to stock of *A. cathartica hendersonii*.

Cultivation Allamandas can be grown in containers or in the greenhouse border. Plants need copious water when growing, but little after August through autumn and winter. Shoots should be pruned back to within one joint of the main branches in January or February. Train new growth close to the roof. Minimum winter temperature is 55°F (13°C). Cuttings 3 inches long can be made from the ripened growth of the previous season and rooted in a temperature of 70–80°F (21–27°C).

Bougainvillea

Commemorating Louis Antoine de

Top: One of the most attractive of climbing evergreen plants for the greenhouse is Allamanda cathartica from tropical regions of America.
Right: The bougainvilleas are handsome vigorous climbers for the wall of a cool greenhouse or conservatory.

Bougainville (1729–1811), a French navigator (*Nyctaginaceae*). Vigorous deciduous climbing plants from tropical and sub-tropical South America, remarkable for their brilliantly coloured floral bracts; showy plants for training on a wall in a large greenhouse. The flowers are insignificant, but the bracts persist for a long time.

Species cultivated *B. glabra*, 5–8 feet, rosy bracts, summer; *sanderiana* is an exceptionally free-flowering, rich rose variety. Both are decorative pot plants trained on wires. *B. spectabilis*, 15 feet, vigorous climber, lilac-rose bracts, March to June, dark green leaves. 'Mrs. Butt' has large, bright rose bracts. These should be planted in a border.

Cultivation Pot or plant out in February in a compost consisting of 2 parts of turfy loam to 1 part of leaf-mould and sharp sand. Prune shoots of previous year's growth to within 1 inch of base each February. Plants require abundant water from March to September, should then be watered moderately until November, and given no water from then until March when growth starts. Winter temperature, 50°F (10°C). Cuttings of young shoots, 3 inches long, should be taken in the spring with a small portion of old wood attached. Insert in pots of sandy soil in a propagating frame with bottom heat. Hybrids may be raised from seed sown in brisk heat.

Clianthus

From the Greek *kleios*, glory, *anthos*, a flower (*Leguminosae*). A small genus of greenhouse evergreen perennials, with handsome foliage and large, showy pea flowers.

Species cultivated *C. formosus* (syn. *C. dampieri*), the glory pea, semi-trailing sub-shrub, 2–3 feet, bright red flowers with a dark purple-black blotch at the base of the standard petal, summer, Australia. *C. puniceus*, parrot's bill, lobster claw, red Kowhai, climber to 10 feet or more, flowers similar but lacking the dark blotch, summer; vars. *albus*, creamy-white flowers; *magnificus*, larger flowers; *roseus*, pink, New Zealand.

Cultivation *C. formosus* is often grown over a wire frame or in hanging baskets. It is potted in spring in a compost of 2 parts of fibrous loam, 1 of peat or leaf-mould, plus some sharp sand, broken brick and charcoal. Careful watering is needed from October to March, moderate watering from March to October. It is difficult to establish seedlings on their own roots but plants succeed if they are grafted as seedlings on to seedlings of *Colutea*, *arborescens*, which are raised

Top: Clianthus puniceas, the Parrot's Bill, is an evergreen shrub from New Zealand, flowering in June.
Right: Dipladenia sanderi, one of the finest of climbing plants for the warm greenhouse. It came from Brazil in 1896

ten days beforehand. After grafting the plants are kept under a bell-glass or in a propagating frame in a temperature of 65–70°F (18–21°C), until union has been made and growth has started, when they are acclimatized to cooler conditions. *C. puniceus* may be grown out of doors against a south or west wall in milder districts without much protection, and in ordinary soil. Elsewhere it will need winter protection as it is frost-tender. It is an excellent plant for the cool greenhouse in the border, in a compost similar to that described above. Propagation is by seed sown in spring in a temperature of 65–70°F (18–21°C), or by cuttings made from sideshoots and rooted in a sandy compost with bottom heat.

Dipladenia

From the Greek *diploos*, double, *aden*, gland, referring to a pair of glands on the ovary (*Apocynaceae*). Hot house, evergreen twining plants, first grown here in the mid nineteenth century, natives of tropical America, bearing racemes of beautiful periwinkle-like flowers opening in long succession. They are slender plants suitable for training up stakes or wires fixed to the structure of the greenhouse, when they flower very freely.

Species cultivated *D. atropurpurea*, 10 feet, maroon-purple flowers, in summer. *D. boliviensis*, 8–10 feet, white and creamy-yellow flowers, summer. *D. sanderi*, 10 feet, rose-red flowers, summer. *D. splendens*, 8–12 feet, white, mauve and rose flowers, summer; vars. *amabilis*, rose pink; *brearleyana*, pink turning to crimson; *profusa*, large carmine flowers, up to 5 inches across.

Cultivation Pot in a compost of rough fibrous peat with a quarter of its bulk of silver sand added. Young plants are repotted in February and brisk drainage is essential, especially if plants are put into a greenhouse border. Plants in large pots or in borders need a top-dressing of fresh compost annually. Summer care against attack from red spider mite is necessary and daily syringeing is required. Water frequently and give liquid feeds throughout the summer, then give only very little water during the winter. Propagation is by cuttings taken in March inserted in sand in a propagating case in a temperature of 70–80°F (21–27°C). These cuttings are best taken from the new shoots formed after pruning, when growth is cut back to within two or three buds of the previous year's growth in February.

Gloriosa

From the Latin *gloriosus*, glorious, referring to the flowers (*Liliaceae*). A small genus of tuberous-rooted, hot house climbing plants from tropical Africa. The showy flowers are carried singly in late spring and summer on

long stalks and have reflexed petals with wavy edges and very conspicuous stamens. All are rather weak stemmed, supporting themselves by tendrils from the tips of the leaves.

Species cultivated *G. carsonii*, 8–10 feet, flowers deep purple, edged yellow, August. *G. lutea*, 6–8 feet, flowers soft yellow, summer. *G. rothschildiana*, 6–8 feet, crimson and purple. *G. superba*, glory flower, 6–8 feet, scarlet, flame and yellow; var. *grandiflora*, yellow turning red with age. *G. verschurii*, 5–6 feet, red and yellow. *G. virescens* (syn. *G. plantii*, *G. simplex*), Mozambique lily, 5 feet, orange, green and yellow.

Cultivation The tubers are very brittle; they should be potted up carefully in January or February in a compost of equal proportions of loam and peat, with good drainage, planting them 2 inches deep, either singly in a 6-inch pot or several in a large pot. A winter temperature of 55–65°F (13–18°C) and a summer one of 70–85°F (21–29°C) is needed, with regular watering until flowering time and a gradual decrease afterwards. Tubers should always be rested during the early part of the winter.

Above: the gorgeous blooms of Gloriosa superba, the Glory Flower.

Lapageria

Commemorating Josephine Lapagerie, the wife of Napoleon Bonaparte (*Liliaceae*). The Chilean bellflower. One of the most beautiful of evergreen greenhouse climbers. The bell-shaped flowers have a waxy, translucent appearance. There is one species only, *L. rosea*, which bears rosy-pink flowers in summer and reaches 20 feet. There are two varieties, *albiflora*, with white, and *superba* with crimson flowers.

Cultivation Although usually grown in the greenhouse, this climber may be grown out of doors in warm southern areas, provided it is given the protection of a west wall. In the greenhouse use a compost of 3 parts of fibrous peat, 1 part of loam and 1 part made up of charcoal and sand. It is essential to give these climbers good drainage; they are best planted into the greenhouse border and trained up wires under the roof, provided they can be shaded slightly in the summer months. Syringe daily and give plenty of water in the summer. They can become badly infested with thrips and red spider if they are allowed to get too dry. Regular fumigation is necessary to keep the plants clean. When growing these shrubs out of doors work plenty of peat into the soil and plant in the Autumn or spring. In severe weather they must be protected. Do not allow them to become dry. Propagate by seeds sown in a sandy compost in spring, in the heated greenhouse, or by layering shoots in the autumn or spring.

Mandevilla

Named in honour of H. J. Mandeville, one time British Consul in Buenos Aires, who introduced *M. suaveolens* to Britain (*Apocynaceae*). A genus of about 50 species of tall, tender, climbing shrubs from tropical America, suitable for the warm greenhouse in this country. One species only *M. suaveolens*, is likely to be found in cultivation. This is the Chilean jasmine, a deciduous climber from the Argentine, bearing sweetly fragrant, funnel-shaped white flowers in summer. The leaves are dark green, about 3 inches long and slenderly pointed.

Cultivation This handsome plant does best when planted in a border in a warm greenhouse in a compost consisting of equal parts of peat and turfy loam with plenty of sharp sand to ensure good drainage. It rarely succeeds when grown in a pot. Maintain a winter temperature of 40–50°F (4–10°C) and give the plant no water from December to February, afterwards watering freely until September, reducing watering thereafter until December. Syringe the plants twice a day from February to July to encourage plenty of new growth. Train the shoots up trellis-work or over the roof of a sunny greenhouse. After flowering is over prune the shoots to within 2 inches of their base. In the mildest parts of the country it may be grown in the open against a sunny wall where it can be given protection in winter. Propagation is by cuttings taken of small, stiff side-shoots about 3 inches long inserted in sharp sand in a propagating frame with gentle bottom heat.

Passiflora

From the Latin *passus*, suffering, and *flos*, a flower, hence Passion-flower, the Spanish Roman Catholic priests arriving in newly colonized South America found in the plants features which they regarded as symbols of the Crucifixion (*Passifloraceae*). This genus of 500 species of tender tendril climbers, mostly from tropical America, has many species with arrestingly beautiful blossoms, and some with edible fruit. The only species

Top: Lapageria rosea, the Chilean Bellflower.
Right: The Chilean Jasmine, Mandevilla, has sweetly fragrant trumpet-shaped flowers.

which may be grown upon a sheltered outside wall in northern areas is *P. caerulea*. There is some disagreement among experts about the colour of the five petals and five sepals. W. J. Bean, the British shrub expert, says they are blue and the American horticulturist, L. H. Bailey, says they are pink, though to the man or woman with normal sight they are apparently greenish-white. About the remarkable circle of thread-like radiating filaments called the corona there is no disagreement; it is purple, inclining to blue. This plant was used by the Spanish priests to give the native 'Indians' a lesson on the Crucifixion as prophetically figured by the leaves, tendrils, petals and sepals, the stamens and stigmas.

Species cultivated *P. alata*, tall climber, flowers fragrant, to 5 inches wide, sepals and petals crimson, outer filaments banded with red, white and blue, spring to summer, Brazil, stovehouse. *P.* × *allardii*, vigorous climber, flowers large, sepals and petals white, shaded with pink, corona deep blue, hybrid, cool greenhouse. *P. antioquiensis* (syn. *Tacsonia van-volxemii*), vigorous climber, flowers 5 inches or more across, bright red, summer, Colombia, greenhouse, but hardy in the extreme southwest, particularly on the Isles of Scilly. *P.* × *belottii*, strong climber, flowers to 5 inches across, sepals pink flushed green, petals rose, filaments blue, hybrid, warm greenhouse. *P. caerulea*, vigorous climber, described above, June to September, sometimes into November in mild autumns, fruits egg-shaped, orange, inedible, hardy in the south and west against warm walls, Brazil; the parent of many hybrids; var. 'Constance Elliott', flowers ivory-white. *P. edulis*, purple granadilla, woody climber, flowers to 3 inches across, sepals green outside, white inside, petals white, filaments white with purple bands, summer, fruit egg-shaped, yellow ripening to deep purple, pulp edible, Brazil, warm greenhouse. *P. incarnata*, maypop, may apple, vigorous climber, flowers to 3 inches across, sepals lavender, petals white or lavender, filaments purplish-blue, summer, fruits yellow, egg-shaped, edible, south-eastern United States, cool greenhouse. *P. mixta*, climber, flowers 3 inches or more across, sepals and petals orange-red, corona lavender or purple, summer, tropical South America, greenhouse or out of doors in the mildest places; var. *quitensis*, differing in minor botanical details. *P. quadrangularis*, giant granadilla, vigorous climber, flowers up to 4½ inches across, sepals greenish outside, pink or white inside, petals pale pink, corona banded with blue and reddish-purple, summer, fruits egg-shaped, purple, 8 inches to 1 foot long, pulp edible, tropical South America. *P. racemosa*, vigorous climber, flowers 4–5 inches or more across, sepals and petals crimson, corona purple,

Above: The strangely beautiful flowers of Passiflora caerulea are typical of the genus. The plant is hardy in some temperate areas.

white and red, stove greenhouse, Brazil. *P. umbellicata*, vigorous climber, flowers small, purplish-brown, hardy in the milder counties against protected walls, South America.

Cultivation The soil mixture for the stove species should consist of equal parts of loam and peat and ¼ part of coarse potting sand. Pot cultivation is quite suitable if a large pot is used, for under-potting encourages the plant to flower rather than produce too much extension of growth. The plants should be pruned in February, removing weak growth completely and shortening the strong shoots by one third. These climbers may be trained up to the greenhouse roof and will stand full sun. The temperature from March to October should be 65–75°F (18–24°C), and from October to March 55–65°F (13–18°C). Water them generously April to September, but sparingly at other times. The greenhouse plants should have a temperature from March to October of 55–65°F (13–18°C) and October to March of 45–50°F (7–10°C).

Passiflora caerulea may be planted in ordinary garden soil, preferably at the foot of a warm wall, though even here a

severe winter may destroy all the top growth; however, some new shoots generally appear later from the unharmed roots. All species may be propagated from seed, or very easily from 6-inch cuttings, rooted under glass in a propagating frame with bottom heat, from April to September. They may also be propagated by layering young shoots in summer.

Pharbitis
From the Greek *pharbe*, colour, in reference to the brilliantly coloured flowers (*Convolvulaceae*). This widespread genus of 60 tropical and subtropical, tall, twining, annual and evergreen plants differs only in botanical details from *Ipomoea* and *Convolvulus*, and the species are often placed in the former genus. Those grown in this country are cultivated for the sake of their colourful funnel-shaped or bell-shaped flowers, usually borne in great profusion. It is a remarkable experience to see, in a large greenhouse, the vigorous growths of *P. learii* mounting to the roof and bearing huge clusters of its large, funnel-shaped bright blue flowers, which later turn to pinkish-mauve.

Stovehouse species cultivated *P. cathartica* (E), to 16 feet, purple, August to September, West Indies. *P. hirsutula*, annual, violet to white, Mexico. *P.*

learii (E), blue dawn flower, 20 feet, blue to pinkish-mauve, tropical America. *P. mutabilis* (E), blue to purple with a white throat in clusters, South America.
Coolhouse species cultivated *P. lindheimeri*, perennial, light blue, Texas. *P. triloba*, annual, pink or purple, tropical America. *P. tyrianthina* (D), shrubby, twiner to 10 feet, dark purple, August to November, Mexico.
Cultivation Stovehouse species grow well in an average potting compost and should be potted between February and April. A temperature of 65–75°F (18–24°C) is required in summer, and between 55–65°F (13–18°C) in winter. Water generously in the growing season, but moderately at other times and prune into shape if necessary in February. Coolhouse species are treated in a similar manner, but do not require so high a temperature in summer and the winter minimum can be 45°F (7°C) though 50°F (10°C) is better. Propagate from seed, sowing the annual species three to a pot in a temperature of 65°F (18°C) in March, or, where the perennials are concerned, by cuttings taken between March and August, and placed in sandy peat in a close frame in a temperature of 75–85°F (24–30°C), or by layering the long shoots. *P. learii* can be grown from its own runners which it drops to the soil at the end of the season.

Stephanotis

From the Greek *stephanos*, a crown or wreath, and *otos*, an ear, a reference to the arrangement and shape of the stamens (*Asclepiadaceae*). A genus of five species of evergreen twining climbers whose stems exude a milky latex if damaged. All are natives of Malagasy. The only species now cultivated is *S. floribunda*, the clustered wax flower, Madagascar chaplet flower or Madagascar jasmine, which produces its highly fragrant white flowers sporadically throughout the year. These flowers are much used in floristry, especially in wedding bouquets. It is a plant for a tropical house where the winter temperature is 60°F (16°C).
Cultivation Plant it in a greenhouse border in a well-drained soil against a wall where support is provided either in the form of wires or a trellis. When first planted it may be slow to grow away but once established it will grow rampantly. Train the shoots as they develop. Once growth really begins it develops so rapidly, twining as it grows that if training is neglected such a tangle develops that it becomes difficult to control. Reduce unwanted and thin shoots whenever they develop, and before growth begins again in the spring, cut back all side shoots to within an inch of the main stems and maintain only enough of these to form a reasonable framework. All surplus shoots should be removed. Top dress annually with well-rotted compost or a dressing of a complete fertilizer. Plants may be grown in pots but they need more attention than do plants in a greenhouse border. After the cuttings have rooted, put three plants to a pot and pot on as each pot fills with roots, finishing, usually, in an 8-inch pot. As the young plants establish themselves in each pot, the developing shoots should be shortened. When the final pot is reached, make a framework either with canes or wire and train the shoots over this. Pinch back all shoots that develop to about two leaves and the sublaterals which form, back to one leaf. Each year cut out some of the older stems and tie in their place some younger ones. Feeding is necessary at regular intervals every year but use nitrogenous fertilizers cautiously and always balance these with potash so as to prevent vigorous growth at the expense of flowering. Mealy bug and scale can become serious pests if control is neglected. Spray with malathion when the pests are first noticed and continue until control is achieved. Propagation is by cuttings which can be taken at almost any time of the year. It is probable that cuttings of young shoots taken in spring as growth is beginning to give best results. Detach them with a heel and dip them into a rooting hormone powder to stop bleeding. Insert them in sand, with a bottom heat at a temperature of 75°F (24°C), either in a closed propagating case or under mist.

Right: Pharbitis tricolor.
Below: Stephanotis floribunda has very fragrant waxy white flowers.

Decorative foliage

Acalypha

From the Greek *akalepe*, the name used by Hippocrates for the nettle (*Euphorbiaceae*). Showy evergreen plants for the heated greenhouse or summer subtropical bedding. Somewhat woody, perennial in nature but usually grown afresh from cuttings each year.

Species cultivated *A. hispida* (syn. *A. sanderi*), fox's tail, red-hot cat-tail, chenille plant, is the only species worth cultivating for its flowers, which are borne in long bright red tassels in late summer and autumn. It can reach 6–10 feet. *A. godseffiana*, 1–3 feet, bears very ornamental leaves (green and white with creamy margins). *A. wilkesiana*, 3–4 feet, leaves coppery-green, marked with red; vars. *marginata*, leaves brown with pale blotches, *musaica*, leaves bronze-green with red and orange patches.

Cultivation Old plants are cut down in February to within a foot of the base and new growth encouraged by frequent syringeing and a temperature of 60–70°F (16–21°C). Cuttings taken with a heel in March strike from this growth. Young shoots should never be pinched or stopped. A suitable compost consists of equal parts of fibrous loam, peat, sand and leafmould. Syringe and water frequently until flowering, then reduce moisture. Summer temperature up to 80°F (27°C), winter 60°F (16°C).

Caladium

Said to be from the Indian or West Indian name (*Araceae*). A genus of tuberous-rooted deciduous perennials from tropical South America, mainly Brazil. The large arrow-shaped leaves are handsome and are borne on stems from 6–18 inches high. They vary in colour from green to cream, some with red markings and patterns, others being bright red. They thrive in a warm, moist greenhouse atmosphere and like plenty of light. They may be brought into the house during the summer, but are not really suitable as house plants for any length of time.

Species cultivated *C. bicolor*, 15–18 inches, a variable species with many good named forms. *C. humboldtii*, 9 inches, light green, centre white. *C. picturatum*, 9 inches, leaves pale on the underside and various colours on the upper surface. There are many named forms of this species. *C. schomburgkii*, 18 inches, green, spotted white, with reddish veins, pale beneath; many striking forms are grown.

Cultivation Pot moderately firmly in February or March, using pots just large enough to take the tubers in a compost of equal parts of turfy loam, peat, leafmould, old manure and silver sand. Move into larger pots in April or May. They can hardly be too warm so long as the atmosphere is moist and there is good light. When the leaves die down water

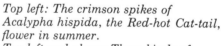

Top left: The crimson spikes of Acalypha hispida, the Red-hot Cat-tail, flower in summer.
Top left and above: Three kinds of Caladium; tuberous-rooted plants, grown in moist warm conditions for their decorative arrow-shaped leaves, that may be taken into the house during the summer.

should no longer be given, and the tubers should be stored from November to February at a temperature of about 60°F (16°C). Propagation is by division of the tubers in early spring.

Calathea

From the Greek *kalathos*, basket, referring to the native use of the leaves in basket-weaving (*Marantaceae*). These shade-loving, warm greenhouse perennial plants, mainly from Brazil, are remarkable for their brilliantly marked leaves. They flourish in a warm, moist atmosphere and when used as house plants the pots should be plunged in large containers filled with moist peat, but a greenhouse atmosphere is what they really require.

Species cultivated *C. backemiana*, 9 inches, silver-grey with bright green blotches, tuberous roots. *C. insignis*, 6–18 inches, light green, purple beneath.

C. lindeniana, 1 foot, dark green with emerald-green zone, maroon beneath. *C. ornata*, 18 inches, much taller in the wild, a variable plant, dark green with pink or cream lines, dark purple beneath. *C. picturata*, 15 inches, dark green, silvery zone, maroon beneath. *C. veitchiana*, 2½ feet, blended shades of green. *C. zebrina*, 1½ feet, dark green with darker stripes, purple and greenish purple beneath.

Cultivation Pot moderately firmly in March in a compost of equal parts of coarse lumps of loam, peat, leafmould and silver sand. Maintain a winter temperature of 65–70°F (18–21°C). Water freely in summer, moderately at other times. Stand the pots on good drainage in a shady position. Propagation is by division in March.

Codiaeum

From the Malayan name *codebo* (*Euphorbiaceae*). Croton. Highly ornamental, stove or heated greenhouse, evergreen shrubs, variegated and colour-splashed, grown for their foliage. This is sometimes broad, sometimes straplike. The one cultivated species, *C. variegatum*, with green and yellow leaves, and which may grow anything up to 10 feet tall, has numerous varieties, including *andreanum*, yellow; *chelsonii*, crimson, orange and red; *evansianum*, scarlet, yellow, green and crimson; *hawkeri*, whitish-crimson and green; *illustre*, yellow and green; *pictum*, yellow, red and green; *tricolor*, cream, green and gold; *weismanni*, magenta, green and crimson.

Cultivation Adequate heat plus humidity is essential. Spring to autumn temperatures should range from 70–85°F (21–30°C) and from autumn to spring 55–65°F (13–18°C). Keep well watered in normal spring and summer weather, when daily syringeing with water is also beneficial. A compost with few added nutrients is suitable. Codiaeums grow well in 5 inch pots. Repot in March, when these are full of root. Propagation is by cuttings of shoots taken with about six leaves, and by leafbud cuttings. Insert in sandy soil in a close frame with bottom heat and temperature of at least 70°F (21°C). Keep them well watered while they are rooting.

Cryptanthus

From the Greek *kryptos*, hidden, *anthos*, flower, the flowers being concealed by the bracts (*Bromeliaceae*). Sometimes called 'earth stars' an allusion to their starfish-like shapes. A small genus of dwarf, tufted, spiny plants from Brazil, suitable for the stovehouse or as house plants. The flowers are mostly white, and borne in a dense tuft of bracts in the centre of the rosette. Mostly they flower in summer. As house plants they are grown for their handsome foliage.

Species cultivated *C. acaulis*, 6 inches, green leaves, white flowers, some varieties with variegated leaves. *C. beuckeri*, 6 inches, leaves mottled green and cream, flowers white and red. *C. bivittatus*, 8 inches, leaves banded with buff above, brown below, flowers white; vars. *major*, larger in all its parts; *roseo-pictus*, leaves flushed pink with cream stripes. *C. fosterianus*, 12 inches, leaves green, red and grey, banded brown. *C. lacerdae*, 6 inches, leaves emerald green, margined and striped silvery grey, flowers white. *C.* × *osyanus*, leaves brownish red, mottled pink and red, white flowers, hybrid. *C. tricolor*, 10 inches, leaves cream, striped green, flushed pink. *C. unicolor*, 6 inches, pale pink leaves. *C. zonatus*, 6–9 inches, leaves banded green and grey, flowers white; vars. *argyraeus*, leaves banded green and golden-brown; *zebrinus*, leaves banded grey and maroon.

Cultivation Pot these plants in March in equal parts of loam, rough peat, leaf-mould and silver sand. Plenty of water and good drainage is needed. Temperatures: September to March 65–75°F

Top: Calathea ornata, a showy plant introduced from Colombia in 1849. There are now many forms.

Right: Codiaeum variegatum pictum, of which there are many forms erroneously called crotons: all are grown for their colourful, ornamental leaves.

(18–24°C), March to September 75–85°F (24–29°C). Stolons are produced in the outer leaf axils, making offsets which can be removed for propagation. When grown as house plants they should be kept dry or nearly dry in winter. In the house they need a light position; the smaller kinds are suitable for growing in bottle gardens.

Dieffenbachia

Commemorating J. F. Dieffenbach, early nineteenth century German physician and botanist (*Araceae*). Dumb cane. Tender evergreen perennials from tropical America, grown for their foliage and used for greenhouse and room decoration. The large oval leaves spread outwards and downwards from the central stem and are spotted or lined with white or cream. The plants are poisonous in all their parts and are said to have been fed to slaves to render them dumb for several days.

Species cultivated *D. amoena*, leaves 1–2 feet long, 6–10 inches wide, heavily marked with cream. *D. bowmannii*, leaves to 2½ feet long, 1 foot wide (smaller when grown as a house plant), mottled with dark and light green. *D. imperialis*, leaves 1–2 feet long, 3–4 inches wide, blotched with cream. *D. oerstedii*, leaves 9–10 inches long, 4½ inches wide, dark green with ivory-striped mid-rib. *D. picta*, leaves 9 inches long, 3 inches wide, heavily marked with cream, but very variable in size and markings; vars. *bausei*, leaves bright green, blotched and spotted with dark green and silver (possibly a hybrid); *jenmanii*, leaves narrower; *memoria*, leaves silvery-grey, margins dark green; *roehrsii*, leaves wider, pale yellow-green, dark green midrib and margins, ivory veins.

Cultivation A rich compost of equal parts of peat, loam and a quarter part of sand and well-rotted manure is needed. Pot in February or March and water freely until September, then water moderately only during the winter. Syringe daily during the height of summer and shade from strong sun. Indoors the plants should not be kept in a bright window. A winter temperature of not less than 50–55°F (10–13°C) is needed. Propagation is by stem cuttings 1–2 inches long taken in spring or summer and inserted in sandy compost in a propagating case. There is a tendency to drop the lower leaves and if the top is treated as a stem cutting in a propagating case roots will soon be formed.

Top: Cryptanthus, genus of stemless plants from Brazil, sometimes known as Earth Stars, are attractive house-plants.
Right: Dieffenbachia picta, introduced from Brazil in 1820, and grown in a warm greenhouse for its ornamental foliage. All parts of the plant are poisonous.

Maranta

Commemorating B. Maranti, an Italian botanist (*Marantaceae*). This genus contains 30 species, all natives of tropical America. One important economic product, the West Indian arrowroot, is prepared from the rhizomes of *M. arundinacea*. However, those species which are cultivated under glass in Britain are valued for the sake of their decorative leaves.

Species cultivated *M. arundinacea variegata*, 6 feet, leaves green and white. *M. bicolor*, 1 foot, leaves olive green, Brazil. *M. chantrieri*, 1 foot, leaves grey and dark green. *M. leuconeura*, 1 foot, leaves green, white and purple; vars. *kerchoveana*, green and dark red leaves; *massangeana*, green and rosy-purple.

Cultivation All need stove treatment and some shade from full sun, if they are grown under glass. They are also grown as houseplants and will succeed provided the room temperature does not fall below 50°F (10°C) and a moist atmosphere is provided round the leaves by standing the pots in other containers filled with water-absorbent material such as peat, which is kept moist. They do best in shady rooms or in shady corners of well-lit rooms. Water in abundance is required from March to October, and plants should be syringed daily during this period. Keep the soil on the dry side from October to March. A suitable compost consists of 1 part of loam, 2 parts of peat, 1 part of sand, in well-drained pots. The temperature from February to October should be 60–70°F (16–21°C), October to February 55–65°F (13–18°C). Repot the plants in spring after their winter rest. Propagation is by careful division of the rhizomes or tubers at potting time.

Pandanus

From *Pandang*, the Malay name (*Pandanaceae*). Screw-pine. Handsome tropical evergreen trees and shrubs, foliage plants with serrated leaves, easily grown, if stovehouse conditions are provided. There are some 600 species in the genus, some of economic value in their native countries, the leaves of some species providing fibres for weaving. The fruits of others are cooked and eaten, e.g. *P. leram*, the Nicobar bread fruit. Most of them are plants of the sea coast or marshland and many have large 'flying buttress' roots in nature.

Species cultivated *P. baptistii*, 4–6 feet, arching bright green leaves with white lines, New Britain. *P. candelabrum*, to 30 feet, large wide glaucous-green leaves, West Africa; var. *variegatus*, leaves 6 feet long with longitudinal white bands on a bright green background. *P. sanderi*, 3 feet, yellow-striped green leaves to 2 feet in length, Timor. *P. veitchii*, 3 feet, dark green leaves bordered with silver, from Polynesia. Other species may be seen occasionally in botanic gardens and the like.

Cultivation Pot these plants from January to April in a compost consisting of 2 parts of sandy loam, and 1 part of equal proportions of leafmould, charcoal and sharp sand. Water freely during the growing season but keep the soil dryish during the winter. Give them a sunny position and a moist atmosphere. The minimum winter temperature should be about 55–60°F (13–16°C). Propagation is by suckers or offsets removed from the parent plant in the spring and potted up in the compost described above. The pots should be kept in a closed propagating frame provided with bottom heat until the young plants have formed plenty of roots.

Peperomia

From the Greek *piper*, pepper, and *omorios*, similar, flowers and foliage are similar to those of the pepper plant (*Piperaceae*). This is a genus of more than 1,000 species, mostly from the warmer parts of America, of mainly trailing plants (many are epiphytic). Some of them have tough thick leaves often with variegation or contrasted veining, and are quite suited to growing in a suspended wire basket. Some species are now used as houseplants, though it helps them to flourish if they can be returned occasionally to the greenhouse for a period. The inflorescence is in the form of an erect catkin-like process, and in some instances this adds to the decorative value of the plant.

Species cultivated *P. argyreia* (syn. *P. sandersii*), thick metallic white leaves with veins dark green, and dark-red leaf-stalks, Brazil. *P. brevipes*, light green leaves variegated with brown, tropical America. *P. caperata*, heart-shaped corrugated leaves, white flower spikes, sometimes branching at the tips. *P. eburnea*, leaves green, veined with emerald green, Colombia. *P. glabella*, trailing red stems, oval-shaped leaves; var. *variegata*, leaves variegated with cream. *P. hederaefolia*, heart-shaped pale grey leaves with olive-green veins. *P. maculosa*, bright green leaves, stalks spotted with purple, tropical America. *P. magnoliaefolia*, thick, cream and grey-green long-oval leaves, rather thick, reddish stems; var. *variegata*, leaves variegated yellow; 'Green Gold' is a cultivar with cream and green leaves. *P. marmorata*, bright green leaves, variegated with white, erect catkin-like flowers, southern Brazil. *P. metallica*, blackish-green leaves marked with

Right: Maranta leuconeura massangeana has green leaves with white veins. They are rosy-purple on the underside.
Below: Pandanus veitchii has leaves spirally arranged around the stems, hence the common name of the Pandanus species: Screw-pine.

white, veins and stems reddish, Peru. *P. obtusifolia*, large, fleshy, dark green leaves to 4 inches long, with purple margins, stems also purplish, flowers white, solitary or in pairs, on red stems, West Indies. P. 'Princess Astrid', a cultivar of unknown origin with small green leaves with a grey stripe down the midrib. *P. scandens*, trailing stems up to 5 feet long if allowed to develop fully, leaves heart-shaped; var. *variegata*, leaves margined cream, leaf stalks pink. This is the form usually available.

Cultivation A suitable compost for peperomias is a mixture of 2 parts of loam, 1 part of peat, 1 part of leafmould and 1 part of coarse sand. Do not overpot; they have a small root system and do not require as large pots as might be expected. The plants should be repotted in spring. Between September and March they should be watered sparingly, and not at all in cold periods. During the growing season they can be given more water, but even then do not require as much as other plants. Keep the plants in a good light, but not sunlight, and in winter give all the light possible. Overhead spraying is beneficial. The temperature in winter should not drop below 45°F (7°C) and 50°F (10°C) is better. In summer they require 60–75°F (16–24°C). Propagation is by cuttings, or single joints with a leaf attached placed in sandy peat and kept close in a temperature of 65–75°F (18–24°C). *P. argyreia* may be propagated by cutting up leaves into several pieces and inserting the cut edges into a sand-peat mixture in a closed propagating frame with bottom heat.

Pilea

From the Latin *pileus*, the Roman felt cap, because of the calyx covering the achene (*Urticaceae*). A genus of about 400 species of tender perennial herbaceous plants widely distributed in the tropics. They are grown in the stovehouse and their main function is as a foil for other plants with brilliantly-coloured flowers or leaves. They are known as the shot plants from their habit of bursting their flower buds unexpectedly and releasing pollen. The flowers are insignificant, and the leaves are delicate and finely divided, rather fern-like in appearance.

Species cultivated *P. microphylla* (syn. *P. muscosa*), artillery plant, gunpowder plant, pistol plant, 3–15 inches, tropical America; the common names refer to the cloud of pollen which is released when the plant is shaken. *P. nummularifolia*, prostrate, small round leaves, good for hanging baskets, South Africa. *P. spruceana*, 3–12 inches, dark bronze-green leaves, Peru, Venezuela.

Cultivation A compost mixture of loam, leafmould and coarse sand in equal parts suits these plants and small pots of 4–5 inches are used, the plants being put in a lightly shaded position in the house.

Potting is carried out from February to April, and the plants watered freely from April to September. The temperature should be 55–65°F (13–18°C) from September to March, and 70–80°F (21–27°C) from March to September. Propagation is by dividing plants between February and March, by taking cuttings from January to May and placing them in small pots in sandy soil in a temperature of 65–75°F (18–24°C), or by sowing seed in spring in sandy soil and placing it in a similar temperature.

Rhoeo

The derivation of this generic name has never been satisfactorily explained since the British botanist H. F. Hance (1827–1886) who named it gave no account of its meaning (*Commelinaceae*). It is a

Right: Leaf cuttings of Peperomia argyreia can be pushed upright into sandy compost and will root quickly. The plant has dark red petioles.
Below: Pilea cadierei with silvery markings on its dark green leaves, makes an attractive house plant.

genus of a single species from Central America and the West Indies. It is much used as a house plant. The species is *R. discolor*, an evergreen plant with erect linear leaves up to 1 foot long and about 2 inches across. They are dark green on the upper surface and purplish below. The variety *vittata* has the leaves longitudinally striped with cream. The flowers are inconspicuous and are produced in small, purple, boat-like containers at the base of the leaves. As the stem elongates, it produces side rosettes which can be detached and rooted for

propagation purposes.

Cultivation Either composts or soilless composts will suit this plant. The winter temperature should be 50°F (10°C), but lower temperatures will do no harm, provided the soil is kept on the dry side. Plants that are cold and wet are liable to rot. During the winter they should receive all the light available, but require moderate shading during the spring and summer. In the home they should be in a well-lit situation, but in one that does not receive much direct sunlight. They like a rather moist atmosphere and this seems of more importance than much water around their roots, although they require normal watering. Once they are in 5-inch pots they will not require further potting on, but will do better if they are given liquid feeds at three-weekly intervals between mid-May and mid-August. Propagation is by cuttings of the offshoots which form at the base of the stems of mature plants.

Sansevieria

Commemorating Raimond de Sansgrio or Sangro (1710–71), who was Prince of Sansevierio (*Liliaceae*). Angola hemp, bowstring hemp. According to modern botanists the generic name should be *Sanseverinia*. A genus of 60 species of rhizomatous perennials, natives of Arabia, tropical and South Africa, and Malagasy, with very thick leathery leaves and rather inconspicuous white or greenish flowers, not often seen in cultivation except, perhaps, in warm greenhouses or stovehouses. Those in cultivation are grown for the sake of their leaves. *S. hahnii* and *S. trifasciata* are popular house plants.

Species cultivated *S. cylinderica*, leaves cylindrical, 1 inch thick, up to 3 feet long in mature specimens, flowers whitish on a 2-foot stem; the raceme can be 2 feet long, August, tropical Africa. *S. grandis*, leaves to 3 feet long, 6 inches across, dull green with darker bands, flowers white in panicles, tropical Africa. *S. hahnii*, leaves in a rosette, about 6 inches long, 4 inches across, obovate with a slender point, dark green, mottled with very light horizontal bands, tropical Africa. *S. trifasciata*, leaves erect, sword-shaped, slightly waved at the edge, usually about 18 inches high and 2 inches across, dark green with transverse bands of lighter green; var. *laurentii*, is the one most frequently seen, it has a golden margin to the leaves, western tropical Africa.

Cultivation A regular brand of compost or one composed of 2 parts of loam to 1 of leafmould and ¾ part of sharp sand is necessary for these plants. With their leathery leaves they are tolerant of long periods of drought and, though they prefer a winter temperature of 50°F (10°C), they will tolerate lower temperatures if the soil is kept very dry. Even during the summer they will take less water than most plants. In the home *S. hahnii* and *S. trifasciata* will do best in a well-lit situation, but will survive in shady positions. In the greenhouse all species require shading in the summer, but full light at other times. Potting on is best done in April or early May. Propagation is by careful division or by leaf cuttings. A leaf cutting of the variegated forms will give rise to unvariegated plants and so these must be propagated by division. It is some time before roots form at the base of the new leaves and they must not be separated before they are at least 8 inches high. If the rhizome can be cut half through when they are 6 inches high, it will hasten rooting.

Left: Rhoeo discolor variegata also has leaves of a striking colour and produces side rosettes in the axils. Below: Sanseveria trifasciata laurentii, growing in a greenhouse border.